D0789406

COUNSELED BY GOD

"Blessed are the pure in heart, for they shall see God."

by
Mark and Patti Virkler

Destiny Image Publishers
P.O. Box 351
Shippensburg, PA 17257

"Speaking to the Purposes of God for this Generation"

ISBN 1-56043-003-6

For Worldwide Distribution
Printed in the U.S.A.

First Printing: 1989
Second Printing: 1993

Table of Contents

To Patti's father, Lyle Hudson,
a man of prayer and faith,
who was called home before
this book was completed,
and her mother, Claire,
a woman clothed with grace and dignity,
this book is lovingly dedicated.

Foreword

"His name shall be called...Wonderful Counselor..." (Isaiah 9:6). When the woundedness of our souls cries out for help, what a blessing it is to turn to our Wonderful Counselor! When our lives are crippled by the bondages of fear and doubt, thank God for our Wonderful Counselor! When the world can only point to our past as a reason for the brokenness of our present, we yet have hope in our Wonderful Counselor!

Our heavenly Father does not expect us to live our lives on our own. He has graciously placed us within a body, a family, of like believers. He commands us to exhort, encourage, love and nurture one another. Whenever we give our advice or opinion to another, we are in fact counseling them, whether deliberately or not. How carefully we must guard our tongues that only the words of the Wonderful Counselor within us find their way past our lips!

A skilled and compassionate human counselor will often be able to help us see our situation from a new perspective. He may guide us to Biblical principles which we have violated, resulting in our present dilemma. Through prayer he may discern the trauma of the past which has left a deep wound in our spirit. But though they may help us find the root of our problem, no human can provide the grace to overcome faulty or sinful habits. No human can pour the balm of Gilead into a broken soul. Counselors who truly bring lasting change and deep healing are those who know how to lead the suffering one to the feet of Jesus where His touch makes all things new.

This small book does not contain the solutions to all of your problems. It does not provide a formula for healing. It does not give foolproof methods of restoration. What it does is suggest that the root cause of the vast majority of difficulties in our lives is losing sight of God and His working in our lives. Jesus said, "Blessed are the pure in heart, for they shall see God." Conversely, it may be assumed that contamination of the heart prevents us from seeing God, and that seeing God purifies and heals the heart. Therefore, the message of this book is encouragement to you to meet with the Wonderful Counselor, experience His touch of compassion, and be made whole. It is only through divine encounter that our lives are changed forever. That is my prayer for you.

Chapter One

Open My Eyes, that I May See

God is reaching out to touch the hearts of His children. He wants to join their spirit with His, to breathe upon them the renewing life of His Holy Spirit. "Blessed are the pure in heart," healed are their spirits, free are they to laugh and dance their way through life, enjoying God and the fullness of His creation. Free are they to love the brethren. Free are they to love themselves. "Blessed are the pure in heart, for they shall see God! (Matt. 5:8)."

If having a pure, healthy, liberated heart involves seeing God, then what does it mean to do so? Where can I look to find Him? Where might I see Him? The Bible offers an astounding array of answers to these questions.

In a Vision

One morning, the prophet Elisha was awakened by his servant with the frightening news, "A great army of horses and chariots has surrounded us during the night. The enemy knows where we are and surely we will not escape. Alas, what shall we do?" What a great way to start the day! Alas, indeed! Do you know that this would be an easy morning to wonder where

God is? It would be understandable if Elisha did not see God in these circumstances.

But what was the prophet's ("seer's") response? " 'O Lord, I pray, open his eyes that he may see.' And behold, the mountain was full of horses and chariots of fire all around Elisha (II Kings 6:17)." In a moment the servant's perspective was changed. In a moment fear became faith, doubt became hope, depression became excitement. Why? Because he saw God!

Imagine for a moment the beloved apostle, advanced in years, bound and in exile on the isle of Patmos. Jesus had promised that He would return, but years had passed with no deliverance. John had given his life to follow his Master, and in return he was alone, far from home and friends, in prison. In the same circumstances, don't you think you might wonder what was happening? Would you begin to doubt that God was really in control?

But what was John's reaction? "After these things I looked, and behold, a door standing open in heaven and the first voice which I had heard, like the sound of a trumpet speaking with me, said, 'Come up here, and I will show you what must take place after these things.' Immediately I was in the Spirit; and behold, a throne was standing in heaven and One sitting on the throne (Rev. 4:1,2)." When John looked, he saw God on the throne, still ruling, still in control, even in the midst of imprisonment, exile, and loneliness.

No doubt there were people sitting nearby who did not see God. No doubt other prisoners and guards saw only the chains, the bars and the thick prison walls. Why was John able to see when others weren't? Part of the answer is found in the words, "I looked." If we are going to be a people who see God, one thing we must do is *look* with the eyes of our heart, in faith expecting to see Him and His movement in our lives and circumstances.

Stephen was another disciple who could have become

angry with God. Stephen had also given his life for Christ and the service of His body. What did he get in return? Execution by stoning. He could have looked at the "disaster" which had come upon him and shaken his fist in anger at God. He could have given in to doubt and despair. God couldn't be ruling, or this wouldn't be happening to him.

Instead, Stephen kept his heart pure, and "being full of the Holy Spirit, he gazed intently into heaven and saw the glory of God; and he said, 'Behold, I see the heavens opened and the Son of Man standing at the right hand of God' (Acts 7:55,56)." God was still in control. Jesus still loved him and was anxiously awaiting his arrival into glory.

One of the Old Testament words for prophet was "seer," referring to their ability to see into the spirit world. Christ has opened the veil that in the New Covenant we may all see what only a few caught a glimpse of in the past. As seers, we can see beyond what is obvious to our fleshly eyes to what is equally obvious in the spirit world. We see beyond the physical reality to the deeper spiritual reality which underlies it all.

In His Creation

Not only can we see God in the spirit world, we can also see Him clearly in the world which He has created. "For since the creation of the world, His invisible attributes, His eternal power and divine nature, have been clearly seen, being understood through what has been made, so that they are without excuse (Rom. 1:20)."

The glory of God is revealed in the sunshine and the rain, in the trees and clouds, in the grass and flowers, in summer and winter. Not everyone sees God in nature. One may look out at the pouring rain and grumble, "I wanted the sun to shine today. Why did this have to happen? I hate the rain!" To another the sunshine is too hot and only adds to the burden of his labor. Yet to those who look, to those who want to see God,

"His invisible attributes, His eternal power and divine nature" can be seen in all that He has created.

In All Matter

Going a step further, not only can God be seen in the beauty and power of nature, He can be seen in every molecule of all matter. "...In Him all things hold together (Col. 1:16,17)." Even matter is alive, infused with the power and life of Almighty God. He is the force which holds all of the molecules together. Thus, when I hold this book in my hand, I can sense the sustaining power of God in it. Not that matter is God. That is pantheism. Obviously God is much bigger than this little book. He is the Creator of all. But all of matter is *infused* with God.

Do you remember what Jesus said when the Pharisees tried to silence His disciples as He rode into Jerusalem? "I tell you, if these become silent, the stones will cry out! (Luke 19:40)." Inanimate though they be, even the stones could be used to praise the King.

In Spiritual Growth

We tend to think that we are responsible for our spiritual growth. But God says that "by *His* doing you are in Christ Jesus, who became to us wisdom from God, and righteousness, and sanctification, and redemption (I Cor. 1:30)." Spiritual growth involves increasing righteousness in our daily living and greater sanctification or setting apart of our lives from sin. I can try to do that by my own efforts but it is only dead works, independent of Christ. True spiritual growth is the growth of Christ within me. I grow in righteousness by allowing Him to be released through me. It is not my responsibility to sanctify myself, but rather my response to His ability to do so. So even when I look at my own life, I can see my God at work.

In Circumstances

When things are going your way, it's easy to see God's hand

at work in your life. When the boss gives you a raise, the car is running smoothly, the children are well-behaved and your wife cooks your favorite meal, how blithely you say, "God is so good! His hand is certainly upon my life!" But what about the day you're fired, the car breaks down (again!), the children are fighting, or worse, have left home to live a life you can't even bear to contemplate, your spouse informs you that she needs "more space to find herself" and your life lies in ruins around you? Can you still see God? Is God still good? Is His hand still upon your life? In the tragedies of life, can you still believe that Christ "works *all things* after the counsel of His will (Col. 1:11)" and further, that He "causes *all things* to work together for good (Rom. 8:28)"?

The nation was at war. The city lay under siege. Months passed with no provisions. Starvation was rampant. Mothers were driven by the madness of the times to eating their own children. Could any circumstances possibly be worse? Could God still be caring for the nation that was His bride? Could He possibly cause the horror and evil of war to somehow work together for the good of His people?

"Yes," the prophet Jeremiah said. Yes, God's hand is still upon you. Submit to the enemy, for God will use all that comes upon you to purify and cleanse our nation. A remnant shall come forth and through that remnant shall come the salvation of the world. Though evil seems out of control, yet I see God still on the throne.

In Everything

"For in Him we live, and move, and have our being... (Acts 17:28)." The pure in heart see God in the very breath that they breathe. They feel His strength in every muscle of their body. Christ is the Center and Circumference of everything. "Christ is all and in all... (Col. 3:11)." He "fills all in all... (Eph. 1:23)."

But how can we see God in all these ways? When my heart

is broken, my faith shattered, my strength all gone, how can I see? Only by revelation. Only by the grace of God can we see control in the midst of chaos, love in the midst of despair, joy in midst of sorrow. We must come to Him, empty of all our own efforts and pray that the eyes of our hearts may be enlightened so that we may know (Eph. 1:17,18). This becomes our constant prayer, to see differently than the world or my flesh see, to see with the eyes of my heart the reality of the world of the Spirit.

David prayed, "Open my eyes, that I may behold... (Ps. 119:18)." David's physical eyes were not blind. He could read the words of the Scriptures. But he couldn't *see*. His spiritual eyes were blinded by doubt or fear or sin. Only the power of the Spirit could cleanse his heart and open his spiritual eyes.

As two disciples walked the Emmaus road (Luke 24:13-35), life had lost all meaning and purpose. Tragedy had struck. Jesus had been crucified, evil had triumphed, the healing love had ceased to flow, life had become purposeless. No longer could they see God. They were "separated from Christ, having no hope, and without God in this world (Eph. 2:12)." As they walked the long road home, they discussed the terrible disaster which had befallen them. Perhaps they discussed their discouragement and disillusionment. After all, they thought the Messiah had come who would deliver them from oppression. They had left their homes and families to follow Him. They thought it was going to be so wonderful, but instead it turned out awful. There was no Messiah, just empty wasted years following a wishful dream.

Suddenly "Jesus Himself approached, and began traveling with them. But their eyes were prevented from recognizing Him." How often the same is true for us. Jesus is right there beside us, longing to comfort and heal, but our eyes are blinded by the brokenness within. And Jesus said to the two disciples, "What are you talking about?" Of course Jesus knew what they were talking about. He knows all things. So why did He ask? Because He wanted to draw them out, to have them express the thoughts of their hearts. Often Jesus will do the same when we dialogue with Him. He will ask us questions and we may want to respond, "But you know the answer to that. Why are you asking me?" But the beginning of our healing comes when we pour out our hearts to God. Don't be afraid or ashamed to let out all your questions and angers, doubts and fears. You will not shock or offend Him. He wants you to bring every negative within your heart to Him that He may touch them and turn them into glorious positives.

But the disciples did not recognize that it was Jesus Who asked them what they were talking about and they responded, "Are You the only one visiting Jerusalem and unaware of the things which have happened here in these days?" He was the only One Who really *KNEW* what had happened! Everyone else only saw what happened in the physical world, but Jesus knew how the physical realm intertwined with the spiritual, how events in one caused responses in the other. Only Jesus found cause for rejoicing in the "calamity" of His crucifixion.

So the disciples poured out their hearts to the Stranger Who responded by explaining how suffering gives way to glory and showing by illuminating Scriptures that God's purposes were being fulfilled, even in the midst of seeming tragedy. How Jesus longs to do the same for you! He longs to open your eyes that you might recognize Him in the dark moments of your life. He wants to set your heart burning within you, exchanging your fear, guilt and anger for His glorious faith, hope and love.

Only God can transform the heart. Only by coming to Him will this purifying take place. Only by doing what the Emmaus disciples did can we be healed. We must not only pour out our hearts to Him but also listen to His response. When circumstances look bad and we wonder if things are out of control, He says, "Be at peace. I'm still on My throne." What seems like calamity to us, is not to Him. Calvary was not a disaster. It was not wicked men out of control, though it looked like that to the eye of flesh. That's what is so marvelous about our God. He is big enough to take the wickedness of wicked men and bring about His best purpose for us. He can accomplish His will for us no matter what man chooses to do. I don't know how He does it; I only praise and worship Him that it is so.

Remember Joseph and the trials which plagued his footsteps, most brought on by the evil of men and women around him? What was his evaluation of his life? "You meant it for evil, but God meant it for good (Gen. 49:20)." Joseph's brothers were motivated by wrath, anger, jealousy and bitterness, yet God used their wickedness to bring about His purposes. You see, God is Love. Love is ruling the universe. And Love is more powerful than any weapon formed against it.

Summary

"Blessed are the pure in heart, for they shall see God." When we see God with the eyes of our heart, in nature, sustaining all matter, in our spiritual growth, in all our circumstances ("good" and "bad"), in short, in everything, our hearts are made pure and whole. But we can only see God by revelation. Therefore we must pray for the eyes of our hearts to be enlightened. We must pour out our hearts to Him, and we must listen to His response. In the next chapter we will briefly review some key principles which can help us to discern His voice more clearly within our hearts.

Chapter Two

Dialoguing with God

In the age in which we live, married so to rationalism and cognitive, analytical thought, it almost seems laughable to hear anyone claim that hearing God's voice is a possible and desirable thing. Indeed, the world has stood by and mocked men of God who claimed to hear His voice, and for the most part, the Church has joined in their skepticism. How far we have come from the Biblical norm, where to know God was to hear His voice! No wonder we have lost God's perspective and are in need of the Wonderful Counselor to set us free.

I have said that in order to have a pure heart, in order to be counseled by God, you must be able to hear the voice of God, see the vision of God, and get His perspective on the situation. Even when we accept this as a worthy goal, it is often not an easy thing to do. In fact, for the first ten years of my life as a Christian, I could not recognize the Lord's voice within my heart and I never saw one vision from Him. As I studied Scripture from Genesis to Revelation, people could hear the voice of God. I wanted desperately to be a Biblical man, but no matter how much I struggled, I could not hear an audible voice within my heart. I thought perhaps I was back-slidden so I repented, fasted and read my Bible more, but still there was no voice. I studied books on the subject, questioned those who were able to hear God's voice, tried all of the suggestions offered, and still there was no voice.

Finally the Lord revealed to me some keys which opened me up to interaction with the Holy Spirit within me. I was able to hear His voice. I was able to see His vision. The testimony of my struggle and a full explanation of what I learned is found in the book *Dialogue with God* [1]. In this chapter I will give a brief summary of the keys which have helped thousands of people enter into two-way dialogue and intimate communion with their Lord.

The keys which I use are found in Habakkuk 2:1,2:

"I will stand on my guard post and station myself on the rampart; And I will keep watch to see what He will speak to me, And how I may reply when I am reproved. Then the Lord answered me and said, 'Record the vision and inscribe it on tablets, That the one who reads it may run [or, That one may read it fluently]."

These then are the four major keys which I have discovered as great facilitators in learning to hear and discern the voice of God:

Key #1 — Quiet yourself;
Key #2 — Tune to spontaneity;
Key #3 — Use vision;
Key #4 — Use journaling.

Key #1 — *Quiet Yourself*

"Be still and know that I am God (Ps. 46:10)." The very first thing I must do in order to hear God's voice is to quiet all of the other voices which are constantly vying for my attention.

Habakkuk said, "I will stand on my guard post and station myself upon the rampart..." In other words, Habakkuk had a quiet place where he could go to quiet his own thoughts and emotions, away from the cares and distractions of life.

I have found several easy ways in which to quiet myself, so I can more readily pick up God's spontaneous flow. Loving God through a quiet worship song is a most effective means for many. When the prophet Elisha was called upon to hear a word from God for the kings of Israel and Judah, he said, " '...Bring me a minstrel.' And it came about, when the minstrel played, that the hand of the Lord came upon him (II Kings 3:15)" and he began to prophesy. In the same way, songs of worship help bring us into an attitude of stillness before God and the divine flow is recognized.

If thoughts come to me of things I have forgotten to do, I write them down so they are not forgotten, and then they can be dismissed from my mind. If thoughts of guilt or unworthiness come to my mind, I repent thoroughly, receive the washing of the blood of the Lamb, and put on His robe of righteousness, seeing myself spotless before the presence of God.

As I fix my gaze upon Jesus (Heb. 12:2), becoming quiet in His presence, and sharing with Him what is on my heart, I find that two-way dialogue begins. Spontaneous thoughts flow back that are from the throne of God, and I find that I am actually conversing with the King of kings.

It is very important that we become still and properly focused if we are going to receive the pure word of God. If we are not still, we will simply be receiving our own thoughts. If we are not properly focused on Jesus, we will receive an impure flow, because the intuitive flow comes out of that which our eyes are fixed upon. If we fix our gaze upon some desire of our heart, the intuitive flow comes out of that desire. Therefore, to have a pure flow, we must first become still and then carefully "fix our eyes upon Jesus." Again I will say, this is quite easily accomplished through quietly worshipping the King, and then receiving out of the stillness that follows.

Key #2 — Tune to Spontaneity

"The Lord answered me and said... (Hab. 2:2)." It is clear

that once Habakkuk had quieted himself, he was then able to recognize the sound of the Lord's voice.

When I was trying to learn to hear God's voice, I listened in expectation for an inner audible voice. Eventually I discovered that normally God does not speak to me that way. Usually the voice of God in my heart comes as a spontaneous thought that appears "out of nowhere" in my mind.

For example, have you ever been driving down the road when suddenly someone's name popped into your mind? Did you take that as an indication that God wanted you to pray for that person? In other words, was that name appearing spontaneously in your thoughts God's voice calling you to intercession? Most people would agree that this is so. It is certainly true for me. That experience helped me recognize that other spontaneous thoughts dropped into my mind were also the voice of God to me. What a revelation!

I began to experiment to see if it were really so. I wrote down the spontaneous thoughts, impressions, feelings and visions which came to me while in prayer and was amazed at the depth of wisdom and the overwhelming quality of love they revealed. Clearly they were not the product of my own mind!

The Bible confirms this in many ways. The definition of "paga," the Hebrew word for intercession is "a chance encounter or an accidental intersecting." Therefore, when God lays upon our hearts the call to intercession, He does so through "paga," a "chance encounter" thought that "accidentally" intersects our minds.

Through my own experiences and the feedback of thousands of others, I now know that it is possible to tune in to those chance encounter thoughts. When my heart is quietly focused before God in prayer, He speaks to me in a gentle flow of spontaneous thoughts, feelings, impressions and visions.

Key #3 — Use Vision

We have already alluded to this principle in the previous paragraphs, but it needs to be developed more fully. Habakkuk said, " 'I will keep watch to see...' Then the Lord answered me and said, 'Record the vision...' " It is very interesting that when Habakkuk quieted himself to hear from the Lord, he actually looked for vision as part of the Lord's response. He opened the eyes of his heart and looked into the spirit world to see what God wanted to show him. I found this to be an intriguing idea.

I had never thought of opening the eyes of my heart and looking for vision. In fact, I had never really considered the place vision might have in the life of a New Testament believer. However, the more I thought about it, the more I realized that God gave me the eyes of my heart for that very purpose. They are not to be used for lust, or visualizing failure or even for pumping myself up for success in my own strength. They are to be used to see in the spirit world the vision and movement of Almighty God.

Theologically, I believe there is an active spirit world functioning all around me. There are angels, demons, the Holy Spirit, the omnipresent God and His Son Jesus. Only the restrictions of my rational culture prevent me from seeing the reality that surrounds me by planting doubt of its existence and neglecting to instruct me on how to become open to seeing it. It was (and still is) God's intention that I use all of the abilities He has given me to enhance our relationship, including the gift of seeing with my heart.

The first step to seeing in the spirit is to *look*. Daniel was seeing a vision "in his mind" and he said, "I was looking...I kept looking...I kept looking... (Dan. 7:1,9,13)." Habakkuk kept watch to see (Hab. 2:1). John was in the Spirit and looked (Rev. 4:1). In the same way, as I pray, I look for Jesus present with me and I watch Him as He speaks to me, doing and saying the things that are on His heart. Most Christians find that if they will only look, they will see. Jesus is Immanuel, God with us. It is as simple as that. We are not inventing something which does not exist. We are merely becoming aware of what really does exist. We begin to see spontaneous inner vision, in the same manner that we receive spontaneous inner thoughts. We can see Christ with us because He is with us!

Often it comes so easily that we have a tendency to reject it, believing that it is only the product of our minds. Doubt is satan's most effective weapon against the believer. If you will persist in recording these visions, testing them as indicated in the following chapter, your doubt will soon be overcome by faith as you recognize that they could only be birthed in Almighty God.

God revealed Himself to His covenant people through dream and vision from Genesis to Revelation. He promised that since the Holy Spirit was poured out in Acts 2, we should expect to receive a continuing flow of dreams and visions (Acts 2:1-4). Jesus, our perfect Example, demonstrated this ability of living out of on-going contact with Almighty God. He said that He did nothing on his own initiative, but only that which he saw the Father doing and heard the Father saying (Jn. 5:19,20,30). What an incredible way to live!

Is it actually possible for us to live out of the Divine initiative as Jesus did? I believe so. One of the reasons for Jesus' death and resurrection was that the veil might be torn from top to bottom and now we all have access into the immediate presence of God. He has commanded us to draw near (Heb. 10:19-22). Therefore, even though what I am describing seems a bit unusual to a rational twentieth century culture, it is demonstrated and described as being a central Biblical teaching and experience. It is time to restore to the Church that which is rightfully hers.

Key #4 — Using Journaling

God told Habakkuk to "record the vision and inscribe it on tablets... (Hab. 2:2)." It had never crossed my mind to write out my prayers and God's answers as Habakkuk did. Yet it is a very scriptural concept. Literally hundreds of chapters of the Bible are demonstrations of journaling; for example, many of the Psalms and prophets and the entire book of Revelation. Why then had I never thought of it? Why had I never even heard one sermon on it?

I called the process journaling and began experimenting with it. I discovered in it a fabulous tool for clearly discerning God's inner spontaneous flow, because as I journaled I was free to write in faith for long periods of time, simply believing it was from God. I did not have to test it as I received it because I knew that when the flow ceased I could go back and test and examine it carefully, making sure that it lined up with Scripture.

You will be amazed as you try journaling. Doubt may hinder you at first, but throw it off, reminding yourself that it is a Biblical concept, and that God is present speaking to His children. Don't take yourself too seriously. Play it like a game. When we take ourselves too seriously, we become tense and block the movement of the Spirit. It is when we cease from our own labors and enter His rest that God is free to move and flow (Heb. 4:10). So relax, get comfortable, take out your pen and paper, and turn your attention toward God in praise and worship, seeking His face. As you write out your question to God and become still, fixing your gaze on Jesus Who is present there with you, you will suddenly have a very good thought in response to your question. Don't question or doubt it at this time; write it down in faith. Later, as you read over your journaling, you, too, will be amazed to discover that you are dialoguing with God.

A Word of Exhortation

I do not encourage anyone to attempt the steps outlined above who has not read at least the entire New Testament and preferably the whole Bible. Further, a working submission relationship to solid spiritual leadership in one's life is essential. We need not fear the spiritual realm, but we must recognize that the Holy Spirit is not the only one who will seek to inject his spontaneous thoughts into our minds. Therefore, all journaling is always open to judgment and testing. First and foremost, it must be totally in harmony with the spirit and the letter of the Word. At no time does personal journaling override the clear commands of God in Scripture. Also, all major directional moves that come through journaling should be submitted to the one(s) over you in the Lord before being acted upon.

Summary

You can learn to hear God's voice and see His vision! No matter what type of personality you have, if you are willing to commit yourself to the task and submit yourself to spiritual guidance with the Body of Christ, a life of intimate communion with God can be yours.

Response

Why not put into practice the principles you have just learned? Write a letter to Jesus, expressing your love for Him, any needs or questions which are upon your heart, whatever prayer you want to offer. When you have finished saying what you want to say, quiet yourself, focus on Jesus, and begin writing the spontaneous thoughts and impressions which bubble up from within you. Praise God that you, too, can dialogue with Him.

Endnotes

1. *Dialogue with God* by Mark Virkler. Bridge Publishing in the United States; Peacemaker's Ministries in Australia.

2. It is strongly recommended that the entire text *Dialogue With God* by Mark Virkler (Bridge Publishing, USA, and Peacemakers Ministries, Australia) or *Communion With God* by Mark and Patti Virkler (1431 Bullis Road, Elma, NY 14059) be studied by everyone interested in pursuing the techniques described in this chapter.

Chapter Three

The Accuser and the Comforter

Have you ever sought to submit every area of your life to Jesus, hoping for peace, power and serenity, only to discover instead inner thoughts of accusation, condemnation and depression? If so, you have unwittingly been listening to satan, the accuser of the brethren.

Jesus is our Wonderful Counselor Who alone can heal the brokenness of our spirits. Often restoration and healing come through a revelation of divine perspective, the ability to see God's loving rule in our life and circumstance. In order to maintain this divine perspective, it is necessary that we be able to see the vision of God and hear the voice of God within our hearts.

We have found that communication from the spiritual realm comes to us in the form of spontaneous thoughts or visions which light upon our heart and mind. We have learned to quiet ourselves and become still that we might know God. We have learned to tune our hearts to receive the spontaneous words and visions from the Spirit. And we have begun to write out our dialogue with God, freeing our minds to receive in faith, knowing that we will have the opportunity to fully judge all that we write at a later time.

As I began to move into a greater awareness of the thoughts from the spiritual world which were spontaneously intersecting my mind, I became aware that not all spontaneous thoughts were compatible with what I knew to be the character of Christ. Could it be that there were messages from other spirits than the Holy Spirit seeking to fill my mind? What should I do? Some people are tempted to retreat before such a realization. If it is possible to hear from satan in the same way that I hear from God, would it not be better to simply not listen to anyone rather than run the risk of deception? While that is one possible response, it is not the course of action which I chose. I had struggled too hard and too long to learn to hear God's voice to be willing to let the enemy steal that blessing from me so easily. I chose instead to become educated, to learn to discern the voice of the Holy Spirit from the voice of the evil one and to stand and fight for the pure voice of the Spirit within me.

Paul exhorted us in the following manner:

"For the weapons of our warfare are not of the flesh, but divinely powerful for the destruction of fortresses. We are destroying speculations and every lofty thing raised up against the knowledge of God, and we are taking *every thought captive* to the obedience of Christ (II Cor. 10:4,5)."

It is apparent that Paul was aware of the spiritual origin and nature of the thoughts which appear in our minds. He was aware that a battle must be fought, enemies destroyed, prisoners taken and authority established in our thought processes. Just because some thoughts enter our minds which are not from the Holy One does not mean we are to stop thinking. Just because a vision lights upon our minds which is impure does not mean we are to shut our spiritual eyes. Rather, we must take charge through the authority of Jesus Christ! Don't surrender without a fight. Destroy the power of the enemy and embrace the power of Christ!

The first step in sorting out the voices that were coming into my consciousness was to become thoroughly acquainted with the character of those who were speaking to me. The words we speak are a reflection of our character. In Hebrew culture and in the Bible, one's name is a capsulizaton of one's character. When you learned someone's name, you learned a great deal about their life and character. When one's character was changed by God, they often received new names. Thus, Jacob became Israel, Simon become Peter, Saul became Paul. Therefore, in order to get an understanding of the character of those speaking to me, I did a study of the names given to satan and to the Holy Spirit in the Bible. My life has not been the same since.

The Names and Character of Satan

The Accuser

The essence of satan's nature is to accuse. The Greek word "diablos," which is translated "devil," literally means "accuser" or "slanderer." The central work of satan is to accuse day and night.

In Revelation we read, "And I heard a loud voice in heaven, saying, 'Now the salvation, and the power and the kingdom of our God and the authority of His Christ have come, for the accuser of our brethren has been thrown down, who accuses them before our God day and night.' And they overcame him because of the word of their testimony, and they did not love their life even to death (Rev. 12:10,11)." Notice that salvation, power, the kingdom of God and the authority of Christ come in our lives when we overcome and cast down the accuser.

If the essence of satan's character is to accuse, whom then does he spend his time accusing? First, as we see here in

Revelation, he accuses the brethren to God. In Job 1:9, satan is
accusing Job before God: "Doth Job fear God for naught?" In
other words, "Of course Job fears you and serves you, God.
Look at all the blessings you have lavished upon him. He only
serves you out of selfishness. He doesn't really love *You*, only
the things you give him."

The accusation of the brethren is not limited to the throne
room of God. Every negative analysis, every critical judgment,
every accusing thought against another which finds its way
into our minds has as its source the accuser of the brethren.
When we cooperate with his evil purposes and speak forth
words of accusation against the brethren, our tongues are "set
on fire by hell" (James 3:6). When our hearts are filled with
demonic wisdom, jealousy, selfish ambition, disorder and
every evil thing find a comfortable home (James 3:15,16).

Satan also accuses us personally, challenging, criticizing
and condemning us in our own eyes. When the Holy Spirit led
Jesus into the wilderness, satan met Him there and said, "*If*
you are the Son of God... (Lk. 4:3)." Can you hear the
accusation in those words? "*If* you are really who you say you
are..." He will do the same thing to us: "*If* you really are a child
of God, why do you act the way you do? If you're so spiritual,
why don't you pray more? Dr. Cho prays six hours every day.
Why don't you, if you think you're such a great Christian? If
you were a good Christian, you would read your Bible more.
You wouldn't get mad so often. You wouldn't do this. You
would do that." On and on the accusations mount in our minds
until we accept the evaluation of us as valid and give up in
despair.

Satan even accuses God to us. Remember, if you will, in the
Garden of Eden, satan (the serpent) said to the woman,
"Indeed, has God said, 'You shall not eat from any tree of the
garden?' ...For God knows that in the day you eat from it your
eyes will be opened, and you will be like God, knowing good

and evil' (Gen. 3:1,5)." Can you hear him challenging the motivation of God, accusing God of selfishly trying to keep something good to Himself? Particularly when we are already tending toward depression and self-pity, this is an arrow which easily finds its target in our hearts. "Has God really said that He loves you? If God really loved you, He wouldn't let such terrible things happen to you. If God wanted to, He could stop those people from slandering you like that. If God loved you as much as He loves other people, He'd give you a better job, a nicer house, a happier marriage. God doesn't really love you at all." If we accept these accusations, if we do not challenge their source and their validity, we are on the path to death, as surely as Eve was.

The Father of Lies

"Whenever he speaks a lie, he speaks from his own nature; for he is a liar, and the father of lies (John 8:44)." Not only is satan the originator of the constant stream of accusation that bombards us, his accusations are a mixture of truth and lies.

For example, look again at the words of satan to God about Job (Job 1:9,10):

"Then satan answered the Lord, 'Does Job fear God for nothing? Hast Thou not made a hedge about him and his house and all that he has, on every side? Thou hast blessed the work of his hands, and his possessions have increased in the land. But put forth Thy hand now and touch all that he has; he will surely curse Thee to Thy face."

Notice that there is some truth to satan's words. God had put a hedge around Job and all that he had. God had blessed him abundantly, making him a very, very wealthy man. So far, satan is telling the truth. Lulled by the accuracy of these words, it is easy to miss the sudden twist, for his next words are a lie. God allowed satan to touch everything that Job had, yet he did not curse God. Sure, he became depressed. He went so far down he cursed the day he was born. But he did not curse God. That was a lie.

Note also that satan's major thrust was to bring into question the motives and intent of Job's heart. Watch out whenever you find yourself making a negative evaluation of another's motives. You cannot know what motivates another person to speak or act as they do. You cannot judge the intent of another's heart. That is God's territory and only He can rightly discern the heart of man. Do not allow yourself to be a passive recipient of satan's lying accusations.

Again, remember that much of what satan says will be true. He is not so foolish as to expect you to accept outright lies. Instead he will mix truth with error in order to make it believable. May I suggest the following approximate equation:

85% truth + 15% error + destructive intent = satanic accusation

---

Begin to look for lies within your own mind. Often they come in the form of generalized negatives: "I can't do anything right." "I'll never make it." "God doesn't love me because of what I've done." "Nobody loves me." "All people are untrustworthy." Recognize that satan is attempting to fill your heart to lie (Acts 5:3). Resist and reject every such negative, destructive accusation.

The Adversary and Enemy

"And the enemy...is the devil (Matt. 13:39)."

"Be of sober spirit, be on the alert. Your adversary, the devil, prowls about like a roaring lion, seeking someone to devour. But resist him, firm in your faith... (I Pet. 5:8,9)."

"He was a murderer from the beginning (John 8:44)."

Satan is unabashedly your enemy. He is seeking nothing

less than your total destruction. Therefore, every destructive, accusing, fear-producing, condemning, guilty, negative thought originally has its source in him. Every idea that leads you down is to be immediately resisted, rejected and replaced with a thought from God.

An "Angel of Light"

Perhaps the most insidious aspect of satan's accusing work is his ability to disguise himself as an angel of light (II Cor. 11:14). While he is injecting thoughts into your mind with the sole intent of bringing you to destruction, he will make you think that those very thoughts are from God. As a result, he will have you walking in constant guilt and condemnation, thinking it is God convicting you while all the time it is satan seeking to bring you to death.

How is such a thing possible? How can we accept the words of the evil one as being from the Holy One? Our enemy is subtle, using even instruments of righteousness for his wicked ends. For example, he will use the scriptures, the very Word of God, against us. He may try to focus our attention on the laws of God and our total inability to keep them, rather than on the resurrection power of Jesus Christ within us which provides all the overcoming power necessary. He will encourage us to use Scripture to condemn and tear one another down, rather than for edification and encouragement as it is intended (Rom. 15:4). We will find ourselves wielding the Bible as a club to judge and belittle rather than an instrument to bring hope and sanctification.

Satan will also try to confuse conviction and condemnation, effectively crippling our ability to either resist him or receive cleansing by the Spirit. However, we need not be ignorant of his tactics. We can learn to discern the difference, cast down the work of the accuser and bring salvation, power and the kingdom of God into our own lives.

- Satanic condemnation promotes a general feeling of despair. It is a vague, over-arching feeling of sinfulness and worthlessness. Holy Spirit conviction points to a specific sin. There is a clear recognition of the exact problem being spot-lighted.

- Satan's condemning voice will urge your destruction. He will try to convince you that the only course of action open to a miserable sinner such as yourself is to give up — on God, on others, on yourself, and ultimately, on life. The Holy Spirit, on the other hand, urges you to repent. Yes, you have sinned, but there is cleansing and renewal through the blood of Jesus Christ. He is faithful and just to forgive.

- Finally, satan will tell you that there is no way out. You are hopeless and helpless and there is absolutely nothing you can do. Your life is a dead end. You have failed beyond all restoration. But the Holy Spirit comes with a specific action which you can take. "Let him who stole steal no more but rather use his hands for labor that he might have something to share with him who has need (Eph. 4:28)." "Put off anger and malice and put on a heart of compassion and kindness. Put off slander and abusive speech and put on praise and thankfulness (Col. 3:5-17)." "Lay aside falsehood and speak the truth (Eph. 4:25)."

We are never to argue against the Holy Spirit's conviction. He will not argue back. Instead, our conscience will become seared and our ears dulled to His voice. However, we must always actively resist satanic condemnation with the testimony of what the blood of the Lamb has accomplished on our behalf, confessing the word of our testimony.

A Thief
"The thief comes only to steal, and kill, and destroy; I come that they might have life, and might have it abundantly (Jn. 10:10)."

Satan is the accuser and source of every evil accusation. He is the liar and the father of lies, mixing truth and error to make us believe the worst about God, others and ourselves. He is a murderer who is always and in every way our enemy. He disguises himself as an angel of light, trying to confuse us and prevent us from resisting his attacks. And he is a thief who is constantly trying to steal, kill and destroy all that is good in our lives. Whenever our faith, hope and love are being challenged or removed, we know who is ultimately responsible: satan! But we do not have to let him get away with his evil plans. We can resist him. We can overcome him. And we can cast him down by the power and authority of Jesus Christ Who lives and rules within us.

The Names and Character of the Holy Spirit

Just as satan comes alongside to resist and destroy you, so the Holy Spirit is called alongside to strengthen you. Just as satan injects his spontaneous thoughts of destructiveness into your mind, so the Holy Spirit injects spontaneous thoughts of life into your heart. Let us now consider the character and work of the Holy Spirit.

The Comforter

At the very core of satan's nature is accusation. The essence of the Holy Spirit's nature is to comfort us with words of truth. "...He will give you another Comforter, that He may be with you forever; that is, the Spirit of Truth... (Jn. 14:16, 17a)." The words the Spirit speaks will be calming, soothing, consoling. Even when conviction and correction are necessary, they will come to us with gentleness and solace. They will be gracious, and full of compassion and hope. They will lift our hearts and bring a breath of life to our broken spirits.

When I became aware of the central nature of the thoughts being dropped into my mind by satan and the Holy Spirit, I began to keep track of whose words I listened to most of the time. Whose words most easily claimed my attention? Whose words found fertile ground in my mind where they could grow and bring forth their own fruit?

I was appalled by what I discovered. At that time in my life, I was listening to satanic accusation, lies and condemnation approximately 80% of the time. I received and gave my attention to the comforting life-giving words of the Spirit only about 20% of the time. No wonder I walked through life constantly feeling condemned, accused and depressed.

We must all commit ourselves to searching our minds, expelling all negative, accusing thoughts and embracing all thoughts of comfort and consolation We must become diligent to take every thought captive to the obedience of Christ. We must not let satan win the battle within our minds, for victory on that front clears the way for control of the very words that we speak and the way that we act.

How specifically can we cast the accuser down from our minds and bring every thought under the authority of Jesus? It is not difficult. It does not take great prayer or faith. What it does require is diligent watchfulness. The moment we become aware of a negative, destructive thought within our minds, we must instantly reject it and replace it with a positive word of truth from the Word and the Spirit. When satan whispers, "You will fail," the Spirit counters, "Have faith in God." Satan says, "You are inadequate," the Holy Spirit breathes, "You have all adequacy through My power." Satan claims, "You are alone," the Holy Spirit promises, "I am with you always. I will never leave you nor forsake you." You *can* choose whom you will listen to. Even when your faith is low and your heart cannot say an amen to the words of the Spirit, hold on to the words of truth. Do not let your emotions determine whose thoughts you will embrace. Hold fast to the word of God and your emotions will eventually be stirred and lifted to praise, comfort and joy.

The Spirit of Truth

We have already touched on the fact that the Holy Spirit speaks only words of truth. While satan is a liar from the beginning, there is no shadow of error, inaccuracy or deception to be found in the Holy One.

"But when He, the Spirit of truth, comes, He will guide you into all the truth... (Jn. 16:13)."

Truth liberates! Jesus said, "...the words that I have spoken to you are spirit and are life (Jn. 6:63)." Satan tries to bind us with his lies. The Spirit of truth sets us free. Lies destroy us. Truth gives us life.

As we read God's Word prayerfully, spend time listening to God speak directly to us through journaling, and abide in His presence, He speaks through the effortless, spontaneous flow within. We must choose to incubate His words of truth that they might bear the peaceable fruit of righteousness in our lives. We must be diligent to guard our minds that only thoughts of comfort and truth be allowed to remain unchallenged. Consider the chart on the following page. Covenant within your heart that the moment you become aware of a satanic lie, such as those in column one, within your mind, you will instantly reject it, cast it down and replace it with the eternal Word of Truth, as seen in column two.

The Convincer

The Holy Spirit is always seeking to comfort us by lighting words of truth upon our minds. This peaceful, gracious nature infuses every aspect of His work in our lives, even when He must speak to us concerning our sin.

"And He, when He comes, will convict (convince) the world concerning sin, righteousness and judgment (Jn. 16:8)."

The word "convict" would be better translated "convince." The concept of conviction usually has a negative connotation in our minds. However, when the Holy Spirit points out sin in our lives, He does so in a totally positive manner. He gently calls us upward to greater righteousness rather than driving us down with guilt and condemnation. He positively draws us to change our mind and our actions through His love and grace.

Satan's Thoughts: Negative, Destructive	God's Thoughts: Positive, Upbuilding
I can't...	I can do all things through Christ Who strengthens me (Phil. 4:13).
I lack...	My God shall supply all my needs according to His riches in glory in Christ Jesus (Phil. 4:19).
I fear...	God has not given me a spirit of fear, but of power, and of love and of a sound mind (II Tim. 1:7).
I don't have faith...	God has given to me a measure of faith (Rom. 12:3).
I'm weak...	The Lord is the strength of my life (Ps. 27:1).
Satan has really got me...	Greater is He that is in me than he that is in the world (I Jn. 4:4).
I'm defeated...	God always causes me to triumph in Christ Jesus (II Cor. 2:14).
I don't know what to do...	Christ Jesus is made unto me wisdom from God (II Cor. 1:30).
I expect to get sick once in a while...	By His stripes I am healed (Is. 53:5). Jesus Himself took my infirmities and bore my sicknesses (Matt. 8:17).
I am so worried and frustrated...	I can cast all my cares upon Him, because He cares for me (I Pet. 5:7).
I'm in bondage...	Where the Spirit of the Lord is, there is liberty (II Cor. 3:17).
I feel so condemned...	There is no condemnation to me, because I am in Christ Jesus (Rom. 8:1).

Satan runs roughshod over your personality, wanting only to dominate and destroy you. The Holy Spirit is always a Gentleman, gently entreating you to set aside sin, to put on righteousness and to recognize righteous judgment. He is the "Spirit of Life," setting you free from sin and death (Rom. 8:2). Satan drives; the Holy Spirit draws. Satan demands, the Holy Spirit entreats.

The Edifier

The comforting words of truth which convince us of sin and righteousness will always result in our edification. If we are obedient to His words, we will never leave the presence of God without being built up within our spirits.

"...One who prophesies speaks to men for edification... (I Cor. 14:3)."

When the Comforter speaks to His Church through prophecy, His first order of business is to edify or build up. Even when pointing to sin and error, the element of instruction and hope will always result in the listener being encouraged and strengthened.

According to the judgment of the Law, we deserve to be destroyed. According to the grace of Christ, we have eternal life. We may be approached, by others and within our own minds, in two ways: 1) with the Law, followed by judgment, or 2) with grace and mercy, through the blood and righteousness of Jesus Christ. We must be diligent to accept only those words which minister grace, life and edification. Further, we must be careful to *speak* only those words which encourage, build up and ignite hope. We have become ministers of reconciliation, not messengers of doom and destruction.

How do you react when you have sinned? Are you able to receive the grace and mercy Christ offers when you repent? Are you able to get back up when you fall and move on in the Spirit? Or must you wallow about in your guilt for a time, bemoaning your sinful condition, mentally flogging yourself for failing yet again?

I have a hard time accepting the forgiveness of Christ. When I have failed, especially in an area which has often been my downfall in the past, I somehow feel that there must be something more for me to do before I can be restored than just repent. How often have I come before the Lord in journaling, crying out in sorrow and repentance. He gently replies, "I forgive you, son." I continue, "But, Lord, you don't know how sorry I am." Again He says, "I forgive you, my child." But something drives me to continue berating myself, unwilling or unable to embrace His cleansing and strength to move on in His righteousness. Finally He breaks through with the words, "Mark, I have forgiven you. Won't you forgive yourself?"

For so many years I lived with guilt and condemnation, mistakenly believing that it was my Father God who was condemning me. It was only through learning to hear His voice that I was able to break free from the bondage of the enemy's lies into freedom and forgiveness. The Bible says, "There is therefore now no condemnation to those who are in Christ Jesus (Rom. 8:1)." I believed in my heart that this was true but it was not a reality in my life. There was condemnation to me, even though I was in Christ! Only through seeing and hearing God within my own heart was I able to recognize the true source of condemnation. When I really got to know God, I found Him to be so much more gracious and forgiving, so much less judgmental than I had imagined Him to be.

The Exhorter/Teacher

"One who prophesies speaks unto men...exhortation (I Cor. 14:3)." "The Comforter...will teach you all things (Jn. 15:26)."

"Exhort" is another one of those words which have taken on a different connotation than that intended by the author and translator. Some seem to think that exhortation is the time to "let another have it," often more closely resembling the work of the accuser than the work of the Comforter.

The literal definition of exhortation ("parakaleo" in the Greek) is "to call a person to the side to encourage some course of conduct, always looking to the future." Notice how close it is to "parakletos" which is translated "Comforter."

Exhortation is thus distinctive in three ways: 1) We call a person to the side. We do not generally correct a person in public. We wait until we can speak in private, if possible. 2) We are encouraging to some course of conduct. We are not simply reciting his errors. Most of us are all too aware of our sin and failure. We do not need another pointing them out to us. What we need is assistance in breaking free from our bondage, specific constructive suggestions that will help us live the life of godliness we aspire to. 3) Exhortation always looks toward the future. We do not wallow around in the past.

A perfect example of proper exhortation is Jesus' response to the woman taken in adultery (Jn. 8:3-11). According to the law, she was guilty and worthy of death. But Jesus went beyond the law and offered mercy, grace and pardon. He spoke one simple sentence to her: "Neither do I condemn thee; go and sin no more." He didn't lecture, moralize or sermonize, as I would be tempted to do. Instead, in those few words He offered pardon, acceptance and encouragement toward wholeness. Again, there was no need to point out her sin. It was ever before her. In the same way, the kiss of love, coupled with the word of exhortation, can often bring healing to our broken lives. And, if we are willing, we can be used by the Spirit to bring wholeness to others in the same way.

If we believe that the Lord wants us to exhort another, we must remember that all exhortation is to be done lovingly (I Cor. 13), gently (Gal. 6:1), patiently (I Thess. 5:14), with great mercy (II Cor. 1:3b) and with a desire to comfort (II Cor. 1:3c). We must "let no unwholesome word proceed from [our] mouth, but only such a word as is good for edification, according to the need of the moment, that it may give grace to those who hear. And do not grieve the Holy Spirit (Eph. 4:29, 30a)."

Summary

In summary, let's look at a Psalm of Asaph, Psalm 73. It is a rather long chapter so I will not include it all here but I encourage you to read the entire psalm, not just the verses below.

Asaph begins: "Surely God is good to Israel, to those who are pure in heart! But as for me, my feet came close to stumbling; My steps had almost slipped. For I was envious of the arrogant, As I saw the prosperity of the wicked..." Asaph begins with a pure heart but suddenly he loses his divine perspective, focuses his eyes on the life-style of the arrogant and wicked, and his heart is contaminated. Instead of seeing God, he sees men. Instead of listening to truth, he accepts the lies of the enemy. As you read verses 4 through 15, it is clear that the father of lies is at work in his mind. There are some facts given: "Pride is their necklace; The garment of violence covers them...The imaginations of their heart run riot. They mock..." It is all true. However, mixed in with these facts are some lies, which Asaph is accepting as truth: "There are no pains in their death... They are not in trouble as other men; Nor are they plagued like mankind..." Not true! From the outside, to the envious eye, it may appear that they are leading a charmed life, but it simply is not so. Asaph is reasoning outside of the presence of the Holy Spirit, and when we do that, we quickly reason ourselves into a hole in the ground.

However, Asaph is wise enough not to remain in that condition. He knows where to go to find truth. He knows that in order to restore his pure heart, he must regain divine perspective. Finally, in verse 17, he begins the process of restoration: "I came into the sanctuary of God..." In the following verses, we read his journaling, the response of God to his complaint and unspoken question. First, God shows him the truth about the wicked. "They are destroyed in a moment! They are utterly swept away by sudden terrors!" In a few words, or perhaps a picture, God brings the light of truth into the darkness of satan's lies and they are undone.

Next God shows Asaph the truth about himself. "When my heart was embittered...I was senseless and ignorant; I was like a beast before Thee..." When I live and think and reason outside of His presence, when I accept lies as truth, I am as senseless as a wild beast. "Nevertheless, I am continually with Thee; Thou hast taken hold of my right hand. With Thy counsel Thou wilt guide me, And afterward receive me to glory." Though Asaph was deceived, though he sinned and lost sight of his God, yet he was not forsaken. When he saw his own sin, superimposed upon it he saw the mercy and grace of his God. No wonder the chapter closes with worship! When we see God and His truth is revealed within, our hearts are purified, communion is restored and joy breaks forth like the morning.

This is the same process we must go through. When we lose divine perspective, when we cannot see God's hand and our minds are clouded by the mixture of truth and error, we too must come into the sanctuary of God. We too must come into His presence, pour out our doubts, angers and fears, and allow Him to speak in response. Only through His voice and His vision can we be made whole.

Response

As you have read this chapter, have you become aware of satan's work in your mind? Have you begun to see more clearly the difference between the voice of the accuser and the Comforter? Have you recognized generalized negatives and outright lies from the enemy which you were accepting and incubating? Have you seen God at work in your life and circumstances?

Take some time right now to come into the sanctuary of God. Quiet your heart, tune to the spontaneous voice and vision of Jesus and write out your questions, doubts and fears in prayer to God. Then make sure you listen for His response and look for His vision. Record what you see and hear. Rejoice in the goodness of God!

Chapter Four

Incubating Only Christ

Have you ever noticed that you can be going happily on your way, enjoying life, praising God, content just to be alive, when suddenly, within minutes or even seconds, anger or depression explode within you and all of your joy is as naught? How can such a dramatic change of spirit take place so quickly? What causes it to happen? Is there anything we can do to prevent it, or at least reverse its results?

As I became more aware of the words of the accuser and Comforter within me, I also became more aware of such sudden "mood swings," and they bothered me. I earnestly sought God for revelation of their source and deliverance from them. Finally, one Sunday morning I knelt at the altar of the church I was then pastoring, crying out for wisdom. There, God brought together the teaching of two great prophets of our time, Dr. Paul Cho and Kenneth Hagin, into a revelation truth which has revolutionized my life, as well as my students'.

I became aware that our spirits have five major senses, just as our physical bodies do. If we are diligent to fill all five of these senses of our spirits continuously and only with God, we will be able to live in the reality of Philippians 4:8:

"Finally, brethren, whatever is true, whatever is honorable, whatever is right, whatever is pure, whatever is lovely, whatever is of good repute, if there is any excellence and if anything worthy of praise, let your mind dwell on these things."

Herein lies freedom, joy and the abundant life which is promised to us as children of God!

What are these five spiritual senses? We have already taken a look at the first two: the ears and eyes of our heart. In addition, our spirits have an inner mind, an inner will and inner emotions. Perhaps you have learned, as I did, that the mind, will and emotions are functions of the soul. As I did a careful study of Scripture, however, I discovered that while these three capacities can be used on a soulish level, they can also be used on a deeper level by the spirit.

It is these five senses which are the fountainhead of creativity within man. It is through them that spiritual realities are birthed into the physical world. These five senses are always functioning, always at some stage of the incubation process. They can be filled by either satan or the Holy Spirit, working either death and despair or life and hope in our lives.

Just as there are three stages in the birth of a child, so there are three stages in the birthing of spiritual realities into our dimension:

Conception:

— Occurs when the inner ear **hears** a word from either satan or the Spirit, and

— The inner eye **sees** a vision from satan or the Holy Spirit.

Incubation:

— As the inner mind **ponders** the word and vision,

— The inner will is set and we begin to **speak** out of that which fills our hearts, and

— Our inner emotions are stirred causing us to **act** upon the word and vision.

Birth:

— In the fullness of time, the spiritual reality becomes physical reality.

How does this work in your daily life? Suppose you come into church on Sunday morning, full of love and joy in the Lord. You look across the aisle and there sits your best friend. You give her a big smile and a friendly wave, but she doesn't respond! Her face seems to be rather stern as she turns her head away from you. Instantly the accuser is at work in your mind, "What in the world is the matter with Sister Susie? She certainly seems to be in a bad mood today. In fact, I don't think she's been herself for several weeks. She never smiles any more. I wonder if she's under conviction! I'll bet that's it. That problem she shared with me awhile ago, I'll bet that she has given in to it and is involved in a pattern of sin. She's probably backslidden! Well, I never did think she was that good of a Christian. She wasn't really such a good friend either, not quite spiritual enough for someone like me."

On and on through the sermon your mind is at work, grasping that accusing word, seeing a vision of your sister's sinful condition and the separation of your friendship, pondering with your inner mind all the negative filth satan has to offer. By the end of the sermon, your heart is overflowing with lies and your mouth has to speak out. You turn to the person beside you and say (with great godly sorrow), "Have you noticed Sister Susie these past few months? I really think she has fallen away from the Lord. She is separating herself from the fellowship of her sisters in Christ and you know what that means. She is deeply involved in sin..." As the poison spills from your mouth, your emotions are churned to the point where you must act on your convictions. As you see Susie slipping out the side door, you gladly avoid all contact with her and proudly make your way to the back door to shake the pastor's hand.

But suppose that when the accuser first spoke his lying words into your heart, you had instantly rejected them, cursing his accusing tongue and turning to Christ to hear a word of truth. What would have been the result? Perhaps the Comforter would have said, "Your sister is going through a very hard time right now. In this hour of trial, she feels I have deserted her. She can't feel my love and because she feels separated from me, she feels unworthy of your love. More than anything else, she needs to feel your love and acceptance today. I want you to be my hands and arms to her. I want you to give her a hug and let her know how much you and I love her."

All through the sermon, again your mind is busy pondering the rhema and vision it has received. But this time, it is bringing love and life to your spirit. As soon as the service is over, you hurry to Susie and speak out of that which fills your heart. As you act out your inner emotions of love and compassion, putting your arms around her, whispering, "God loves you so much, and so do I," healing tears begin to flow, friendship is restored and her faith is renewed.

The choice is ours. Who will we listen to? Whose words will we ponder? Whose emotions will fill us and compel us to speak and act? Will we be ministers of condemnation or reconciliation? Will we bring pain or healing to those we touch?

One more example: Suppose your boss offers you a promotion. It will mean greater responsibility and require learning some new skills. Instantly the enemy whispers, "You don't want that job! You don't need that kind of hassle.

Everything is going fine the way it is. Don't make waves for yourself. If you take that position, people will be depending on you more. If you mess up, everyone will know and blame you. And you know you *will* mess up. You're too old to learn anything new. It's too hard. You just can't do it."

As you talk it over with your wife that night, the picture of failure grows larger and larger. Not only will you cause problems in your department, you'll make the whole company lose money. They'll end up going bankrupt, you'll lose your job and the respect of all your friends, because they will all know it is your fault the company folded. Fear grips your heart and the next morning you tell your boss, "No thanks. I'm satisfied right where I am."

But what if you rejected the liar's words the instant they appeared in your mind? What would the Spirit say instead? Perhaps He would whisper, "How wonderful to have an opportunity to continue to grow and learn new things! You are filled with My strength and wisdom, so you will be able to become skilled in this new area of responsibility. If you put your trust in Me and meditate upon my word, I shall make your way successful. You can do anything because My strength fills your life." A vision of success fills your mind, and as you ponder the words of life, you determine in your spirit to do your best through Christ and gratefully you accept the new position.

I hope that you are beginning to grasp the consistency with which this chain of events takes place within our spirits. Whether we are aware of it or not, our hearts are constantly in the process of creating and bringing forth into the third dimension that which was conceived in the spiritual realm. Therefore, it is imperative that we present the eyes and ears of our hearts only to Christ to be filled by Him that the peaceable fruit of righteousness may be born through us.

Jesus said, "The lamp of your body is your eye; when your

eye is clear, your whole body is also full of light; but when it is bad, your whole body is full of darkness (Luke 11:34-36)". The eyes of our heart are one of the most powerful tools for good and evil which God has created within us. I believe that the focus of our inner eyes provides the most powerful dynamic of our lives. We are told to "fix our eyes on Jesus, the author and perfecter of our faith (Heb. 12:2)." Only by focusing our inner eyes on Jesus can our eyes be clear and our whole body be full of light. If we do not deliberately offer them to Christ to be filled with His divine light, they will automatically be filled by satan bringing the darkness of lust, fear, failure and inadequacy to our whole bodies.

Once we have heard God's word and seen His vision, we must incubate it within our spirits, allowing our inner mind, inner will and inner emotions to become saturated with it. We thus become pregnant with the purposes of God and carriers of His sovereign power in the world. Our inner mind ponders only God's thoughts, never the doubts and negativism of satan. We choose with our inner will to speak forth with faith that which God has spoken. As our inner emotions are charged with the vision of God, they motivate us to move out and act in faith upon God's glorious promises, expecting a miracle. In the fullness of God's timing, not ours, He will bring forth His promise, giving glory to His name. To make sure we are not eligible to receive any of the glory, He will wait until we have stopped trying to bring His promises into being in our own strength. When it is totally evident to all that it cannot be done in the natural, He will do it supernaturally.

Abraham, the Father of Faith

Abraham is a classic example of this experience. In Gen. 12:2, God spoke a rhema word into Abram's heart, "I will make you a great nation." What a glorious promise! What a positive, edifying, joyful word! As you work with journaling and hearing God's voice, you, too, will find that God's words are glorious, positive, edifying and joyful. He will promise to do great things through you, too. Satan will try to steal these words of truth with his accusations, "God can't use you. Look who you are." But the Spirit breathes back into our condemned and discouraged hearts, "I will use you. Look at Who I AM!"

Eleven years later, Abram had another visit from the Lord. This time, God showed him the stars of the sky and the sands of the seashore in a vision. "So shall your descendants be," He said. Here stands Abram, 86 years old and childless. How does he respond to such an amazing promise? "Then he believed in the Lord..." Abram must have believed the rhema word which came to him so many years before because he acted in obedience to it. However, the faith that came as a result of vision was so deep and powerful that it was worthy of comment in the Word. Such is the power of vision. It solidifies the promise, giving substance to that which cannot be seen in the natural.

Having received both word and vision, Abraham filled his inner mind with only thoughts of faith.

> "In hope against hope he believed...not being weak in faith, he considered not his own body...He staggered not at the promise of God through unbelief; but was strong in faith...And being fully persuaded that, what He had promised, He was able also to perform... (Rom. 4:17-22)."

Though years went by without seeing the physical manifestation of the promise of God, Abraham did not falter in faith but filled the mind of his heart with the words and vision He had received from the Lord.

Thirteen more years passed without the birth of a child. Finally, God appeared again with a command to Abram, "Your name shall be Abraham, For I will make you the father of a multitude of nations (Gen. 17:5)." In other words, every time Abraham said his name from this time forth, he would be confessing his faith in the word of God. "Hello, I am a father of a multitude." "How many children do you have?" "Well, none yet, but God has promised!"

It is important to notice at what point the command for confession came. Abraham had been pondering the word and vision of God for twenty-four yeas. He had conceived, he had incubated, he was pregnant with the promises of God! When we confess words of faith, we sound foolish to the unbelieving world and are often mocked and criticized as a result. If this happens when the seed is small and has not yet been firmly established, it is easy to abort the vision and abandon the word. But if persecution comes against us when we are near full-term, we have the strength to say, "*I know* this is true. This word has been growing inside of me and it's ready to explode into this world. Nothing can make me silence my confession!" Confession is a vital part of the creation process, but obeying God's word concerning *when* to confess is just as important as *what* to confess.

God also gave Abraham the command of circumcision when he was 99 years old (Gen. 17:10-24). No mention had been made about conditions of the covenant up to this point. However, Abraham's inner emotions were so attuned to the Spirit that he was moved to immediate obedience. "In the very same day Abraham was circumcised... (Gen. 17:26)." Notice that the Lord continued to give Abraham instructions concerning his preparation for the miracle during the incubation stage. In the natural, an expectant mother does many things to prepare for the birth of her child. She has good medical care, eats carefully and nutritiously, takes giant vitamin pills, does exercises, prepares her mind and body for the delivery, and arranges a special room for her little one. In the same way, we must do certain things to prepare for the birth of the vision in our lives. God will tell us what to do and when to do it. We must only be immediately obedient to His word. It is not good enough to say, "God promised this to me twenty years ago." You must know what He is saying about that promise today.

Finally, after twenty-five years of waiting, there came forth the creative power of God and Isaac was born. However, that is not the whole story. During the time of waiting, Abraham made one mistake: "Abram listened to the voice of Sarai (Gen. 16:2)." It was understandable. A long time had passed since the promise had come. Perhaps God was waiting for them to do something different. Perhaps it was time for a committee meeting to see how they could help God accomplish His goals. So Abraham forgot the voice of God for a moment and listened instead to earthly wisdom. The next time God came to speak to him, he proudly pointed to the results of his efforts and said, "Oh that Ishmael might live before Thee! See what we did, Lord? We made a child, just like you said You would. Isn't that good enough? Isn't that the fulfillment of your promise?" "But God said, 'No...' (Gen. 17:18,19)." Our efforts cannot achieve God's goals. As long as we try to make it happen, our effort becomes a hindrance and the vision remains unfulfilled. Only when our efforts are exhausted and all natural hope is gone can God supernaturally move, fulfill His promise and bring glory to Himself.

Summary
The chart at the end of this chapter summarizes the ideas presented in it. The process is constant. It is up to us to determine whose voice and vision we will allow to be birthed through us.

Response
It is important that you give God a chance to apply the truths you are taught to your own life. If you actually hope to be counseled by God, you must meet with Him, talk to Him and listen to Him. Take up your journal and go to a quiet place where He can reveal Himself to you. What dreams has He

Incubating Only Christ
By filling all five senses of the heart with Him

	SENSE	HOW USED	BIBLE EXAMPLE	STAGE
1.	Inner Ear (Jn 5:30)	Receives God's Rhema	Gen 12:1-3	CONCEPTION
2.	Inner Eye (Rev 4:1)	Receives God's Vision	Gen 15:5,6	CONCEPTION
3.	Inner Mind (Lk 2:19)	Ponders God's Thoughts	Rom 4:20,21	INCUBATION
4.	Inner Will (Acts 19:21)	Speaks on God's Rhema	Gen 17:5	INCUBATION
5.	Inner Emotions (1 Kings 21:5)	Acts on God's Rhema And Vision	Gen 17:23	INCUBATION
END RESULT		Death of the Vision "I" am unable to Bring it about	Gen 16:2 Gen 17:18,19	BIRTH
END RESULT		Supernatural resurrection of the Vision. "In the fullness of Time GOD brings it forth."	Gen 21:1,2 Gal 4:4a	BIRTH

"Fixing our eyes on Jesus, the author and perfecter of our faith." (Heb. 12:2)

"I am the Alpha and the Omega, the first and the last, the beginning and the end." (Rev. 22:13)

Chapter Five

Seeing God in the Past

"Blessed are the pure in heart, for they shall see God." But what about those times when I can't see God? What about those horrible experiences in my past which so traumatized me that I am still affected by them today? What about the times that were so awful, I just know God wasn't there? How can my heart be cleansed and healed of the wounds I received even before I knew Christ?

Only Our Wonderful Counselor Who lives outside of time can be with us simultaneously in the present and the past. Christ is the eternal I AM. He is never "I was" nor "I will be," but only "I AM," forever in the now of time. He exists beyond time; it has no power to limit Him. It is just as easy for Him to be present at a moment in your past as it is for Him to be present right here and now. Indeed, He *is* present in your past at the same time as He is present in your now and in your future. He is everywhere and always here. He is the God of the here and now, and every moment of time is to Him, at every moment, the here and now. These concepts are too big for our minds to comprehend but they are nonetheless true.

Because they are true, because Christ is omnipresent and lives in timelessness, He is able to minister total healing to every hurt of our past. This experience is called by various names: inner healing, healing of memories, deep healing, or healing of the soul. The name doesn't matter, except as a way of capsulizing several truths of Scripture. Essentially, deep hurts of the past are healed through forgiveness and allowing Christ to walk through the scene with healing love.

There are several things inner healing is not. 1) It is not *you* drumming up hurts to be healed. We do not scour our memories and dredge up every negative experience we can find. It is *Christ* gently bringing to our consciousness an experience that He wants to touch. 2) Inner healing is not you manufacturing a new scene. New Age teaching has a form of inner healing in which one replaces in his memory the words or actions which hurt him with ones of love and kindness. Such a restructuring of the past is never the work of the Holy Spirit because it is built on lies, and He can never lie. Instead, true inner healing occurs when we *see Christ* moving freely within the scene as it actually happened. 3) Inner healing is not a list of formulas, even though I may present it that way. Inner healing, like all counseling by God, is a living encounter with a living God.

Many excellent books have been written on inner healing, especially in recent years. I highly recommend *Healing for Damaged Emotions* by David Seamonds and *You Can Be Emotionally Free* by Rita Bennett to everyone who is interested in a greater understanding of this ministry. Certainly I cannot say all that should be said on the subject in one short chapter. Instead I will simply give an overview of the process as illustrated in the ministry of Jesus in the Gospel of John.

The story begins on the night before Jesus' crucifixion. Peter, strong, dynamic, and impetuous, had made an attempt to defend his best Friend. Wielding a sword as the soldiers attempted to take Jesus away, he had managed to cut off one man's ear. But instead of receiving commendation and gratitude, Jesus had rebuked him and restored the ear. Now Jesus was on trial before the high priest and there seemed to be nothing Peter could do. He waited in the courtyard for some word, not wanting to be too far from his Master.

As he sat with the others in the courtyard, warming himself by a charcoal fire, a servant girl announced, "You too were with Jesus the Galilean." Fearfully he denied the fact and moved away from the girl. Before long, another servant repeated the charge and again Peter denied that he even knew Jesus. Finally, a bystander claimed, "The way you talk gives you away. You must be one of His followers." Immediately Peter changed the way he talked and began to curse and swear, saying, "I do not know the man!" As the cock announced the arrival of a new day, Peter went out and wept bitterly. No other time in Scripture does it speak of Peter weeping. Clearly this was a deeply wounding event in his life. In fact, as a result, he turned his back on his call to ministry and returned to his former employment.

Several days passed. Jesus appeared to many of His disciples in many places. He even went to the shore of the Sea of Galilee where a big burly fisherman was trying to put the past behind him and get on with his life. Just as the day was breaking, Jesus appeared to him and his friends who were fishing together. He prepared them a breakfast of fish and bread over a charcoal fire. After they had eaten, Jesus began to question Peter, "Simon, son of John, do you love me?" Peter replied, "Yes, Lord, you know I love you." Jesus responded, "Tend My lambs." Again, Jesus asked him the same question, Peter gave the same reply and Jesus responded in a similar way. And again a third time, the conversation was repeated.

What was the point of this whole encounter? I am convinced that Jesus was ministering inner healing to the deep

wounds Peter had experienced as a result of his three-fold
denial of Christ. Notice the correlation of the following chart:

	The Steps Taken	A Biblical Example (Peter: Matt. 26:69-75/Jn. 21:2-17)
1.	Using vision, go back and re-enter the hurt.	Charcoal fire Dawn Three-fold confession
2.	Using vision, bring Jesus into the scene.	"Jesus stood on the beach..." (Jn. 21:4-15)
3.	Using vision, let Jesus move freely, healing the hurt with His loving presence.	Jesus' statements of affirming love. Tend My lambs Shepherd My sheep Tend My sheep

Let's discuss each step of the inner healing process and see
how it was applied to Peter.

1) Using vision, go back and re-enter the hurt. It is
important that you actually see the scene and feel at least a
small portion of the emotions you felt at the time. Don't
become so involved in the emotions that you are again unable
to see Christ there. If the experience was too emotional and
traumatizing, Jesus may choose to take you to a scene soon
after the event instead. However, the use of vision is essential.

Notice how Jesus re-set the scene of Peter's pain for him: It
happened just as day was breaking. It happened beside a
charcoal fire. (These two passages are the only times a
charcoal fire is mentioned in the New Testament.) And it
involved a three-fold confession.

2) Using vision, invite Jesus to reveal Himself in the scene.
Healing only takes place when we are touched by Jesus. He
was actually there when the painful event took place. We may
think, "It was too awful! He couldn't possibly have been
there." Yet the Psalmist David says, "Even if I am in Hades,
You are with me there." There is no place and no experience
so bad that He is driven from our side. We are simply asking

our eyes to be opened that we might see what He was doing and what He wanted to do if we had allowed Him to.

In John 21:4-15, "Jesus stood on the beach..." He came to Peter and entered the scene of his failure and pain.

3) Using vision, let Jesus move freely, healing the hurt with His loving presence. Again I must say, we are not manufacturing false visions. Jesus was actually there in our painful experiences. It was only our blindness or over-whelming emotions which hid Him from our sight. He was working and moving, even though we could not sense His presence. Now, as our eyes are open, we see Christ and are healed. I hesitate to even offer suggestions about what we may see Him doing, for He is so creative that the possibilities are limitless. I can say quite confidently that He probably won't do what you expect Him to do. From this detached distance, we can say, "He might do this or say that." But such theories do not bring healing to our souls. Only experiencing the living Christ can set us free.

There are many truths to be found in Jesus' conversation with Peter but we will zero in on just one. What was Jesus' response to Peter's confessions of love? "Tend My lambs; Shepherd My sheep; Feed My sheep." In other words, Jesus was saying, "I forgive you, Peter. I accept you and I want you to carry on with the ministry which I have given you. You are totally restored."

Couldn't Jesus have simply shaken Peter's hand and said, "I forgive you, Peter. Carry on?" Why go to all the trouble of re-setting the scene of his pain? Because *spirit-level emotions do not respond to cognitive facts.* The spirit speaks the language of pictures and only through vision can the spirit be touched and healed.

Summary

Through the ministry of Jesus which we call inner healing, we are able to see Christ even in the midst of painful experiences of our past. As we offer the eyes of our heart to Him, asking Him to reveal His presence and work in these events, He will often call upon us to forgive those who were responsible for our pain. Not that we in any way condone their words or actions, but through forgiveness, we are set free to receive forgiveness and healing from God. Those who wounded us are also set free by our forgiveness to also be touched by the healing power of the Spirit of Christ.

Response

Inner healing can happen in many different ways. Often it happens at the altar when we pour out our hurt and anger before the Lord. He gives us revelation and divine perspective and we come away healed and restored. For me, inner healing frequently happens as I journal. After I have expressed my feelings to the Lord, He responds with love and grace and, again, divine perspective is restored. Much inner healing takes place "naturally" (supernaturally) as a result of our growth in the Lord. Increase in knowledge and understanding and a deeper experience in Him produce healing.

Inner healing can also take place as one or two individuals pray with us. This is especially effective when we run into road blocks which prevent us from letting Christ complete the work.

If you have become aware of a need for inner healing in your life, I recommend that first you go to the Lord directly through journaling. Remember to use vision throughout the experience. Record in your journal all that takes place in your heart. If you are unable to find release on your own in this way, you should go to someone who has an established prayer ministry of inner healing, someone whom you know has a respected reputation.

Our Wonderful Counselor wants to set you free from all the angers, hurts, disappointments, bitterness, fear and failure of the past which bind you and rob you of your joy in Him. When you see Him in the midst of every experience of your life, your heart will be healed.

Chapter Six

From Fear to Faith

Probably the most paralyzing emotion which can overwhelm us is fear. No other emotion can so effectively negate our faith, stifle our joy, disrupt our peace and manacle our walk with the Lord. Fear is such a pervasive emotion in our society that many centers have been established all over the nation for the sole purpose of helping individuals overcome, or at least learn to live with, their fears. Many different methods are used to bring release from the bondage. In this chapter, we will examine only one: moving from fear to faith by hearing a rhema word from God.

"There is no fear in love; but perfect love casts out fear... (I Jn. 4:18)." Jesus came to heal us of our fear. Fear is the result of the incubation of satan's mendacious evaluation of life. Faith is the result of the incubation of the Lord's perspective which is full of grace and truth.

Fear is not simply a psychological problem. It's root is in satanic rhema, which makes it a spiritual problem. The Bible says:

"...the weapons of our warfare are not of the flesh, but divinely powerful for the destruction of fortresses. We are

destroying speculations and every lofty thing raised up
against the knowledge of God, and we are taking every
thought captive to the obedience of Christ (II Cor.
10:4,5).''

Paul clearly teaches that our thought processes are to a
large extent of a spiritual nature. Therefore, when our minds
receive a negative thought which lures us into the pattern of
fear, we are involved in a spiritual warfare which can only be
won by spiritual means. Fear is destroyed by replacing satan's
rhemas with God's.

What is it that we fear and worry about? Studies have
indicated that as many as 92% of our worries are unjustified,
either because they involve things that will never happen,
things in the past that can't be changed through worry, or
petty, unimportant things which do not warrant the effort. If
you will examine your own worries, you will probably find this
is true for you as well. Therefore, the vast majority of your
worrying is a waste of time and energy, and is in fact time
spent building the kingdom of darkness. Remember that worry
is a form of incubation and eventually that which grows within
us must be delivered into the physical world in some form.

However, even the 8% of our worries which might be
considered legitimate causes for concern should not bring
negativism and fear into our hearts and minds. If these issues
are indeed important items that should be considered, how
should they be handled, if not with worry?

"Be anxious for **nothing** but in everything by prayer and
supplication with thanksgiving let your requests be made
know to God (Phil. 4:6)."

Here then is the solution to fear and worry: prayer plus
supplication plus thanksgiving equals freedom.

Perhaps you have heard that formula before. Perhaps you
have even tried it and found it an empty, meaningless ritual.
You are right; it is empty and meaningless, *unless* in the midst

of your prayer, you contact the Wonderful Counselor and hear His words of rhema to you on the subject. Mechanical formulas do not heal spiritual wounds. Academic exercises do not set the spirit free from its bondage to lies. Only a living encounter with the living Christ can transform your heart of fear to a heart of faith.

Therefore, the "formula" or steps to moving from fear to faith are actually:

1) With prayer and supplication, make your needs known to the Lord. Pour out all the needs, concerns and worries which are holding your mind captive.
2) Quiet yourself in the presence of God.
3) Receive revelation from God. Hear His words and see His vision of life.
4) Respond with worship and thanksgiving. You won't need to be reminde ! to do this. It will be the automatic response of your heart to the healing presence of Christ.

Let us examine a Biblical example of this process. Psalm 61 is a psalm of David which begins with a heart of fear and ends in worship.

"Hear my cry, O God; Give heed to my prayer. From the end of the earth I call to Thee, when my heart is faint; Lead me to the rock that is higher than I...Let me dwell in Thy tent forever; Let me take refuge in the shelter of Thy wings (vs. 1-4)."

David is crying out to the Lord for shelter and defense. His heart is fainting with fear. He feels he is far from God, even to the end of the earth, yet he knows that God has been his protection in times past. So he comes before the Lord and pours out his feelings and his request.

At the end of verse 4, we see a Hebrew word, *Selah*. The New American Standard Bible indicates that this means "a pause, a crescendo, or a musical interlude." When David had finished expressing all his negative feelings to the Lord, he stopped talking and quieted himself in the Lord's presence while music continued to play to help him remain still. This is the place we so often miss the power of prayer. How quick we are to run into the sanctuary, blubber out our prayers and run away again. No wonder our prayer times become empty, dry rituals. We have missed their purpose entirely. Prayer is not to be a monologue, but a dialogue, two people sharing back and forth, conversing about the things on both of their hearts. If we are going to be healed and delivered of our fear, we must not only express our feelings to the Lord, but we must then stop talking and give Him a chance to respond.

The change in David's heart as a result of this quiet musical interlude is strikingly clear in the rest of the psalm.

"For Thou *hast* heard my vows, O God; Thou *hast* given me the inheritance of those who fear Thy name. Thou *wilt* prolong the king's life; His years *will* be as many generations. He *will* abide before God forever... (vs. 5-7, emphasis added)."

There is clearly a new sense of confidence in David's spirit. These are strong declarations of faith based on the revelation of God within his heart. No more is he bound by fear but now he fairly leaps with faith.

It is no wonder that the psalm ends with praise, worship and obedience. When we have heard from the Lord and He has replaced our fear with faith, no one will need to exhort us to praise. No one will be able to keep us from it!

Again I must repeat that this is not an academic process. You can't talk yourself out of fear intellectually, because it is not mental but spiritual at its roots. Faith must well up from within you as a result of encounter with Jesus Christ in order to be set free from fear.

In using this process, it is important to remember that we are not attempting to drive out the darkness of fear. We cannot force the darkness from our minds by our own efforts any more than we can push the darkness from a room with our hands. Instead, we are bringing light into the dark place and instantly the darkness flees.

Neither are we trying to empty our minds of fear. An empty mind is never the goal of the Spirit of God. In fact, we do not focus on the fear at all. Perhaps you have found that the more you focus on something, the greater it looms within your mind, even if your focus is on trying to avoid it. For example, if you are dieting, you may try not to think about hot fudge sundaes. The more you think about not thinking about them, the bigger the desire for them grows within you. Temptation and sin cannot be conquered by direct attack. Instead, we overcome by replacement. Instead of focusing on hot fudge sundaes, see yourself slim, healthy and full of vitality. Instead of focusing on emptying your mind of fear, fill up your mind with faith. Hold on to that rhema word and vision you have received from Christ. Let it roll around and around in your mind and heart. Meditate on it day and night. Incubate His truth until it is birthed into your existence.

Finally, we are not *coming against* the fear. Even though it is something evil which we are attacking, still a negative stance is always destructive. Instead, we are *coming unto* God in a positive action that He might speak life to our souls.

How can God speak words of rhema which will bring us peace? There are many ways. He may speak through the illumined Word (Eph. 1:17,18). As we meditate on the Scriptures, His message may suddenly leap off the page and into our hearts. He may also speak with a still small voice (I Kings 19:12,13), in the spontaneous thoughts and impressions which come as we are quiet before Him.

God has promised to speak to us through dreams and visions (Num. 12:6). In our culture, dreams have been dismissed as simply yesterday's leftover lasagna, and visions as the escape attempts of an unstable mind. But that is not God's view. He has promised that He would give wisdom and knowledge to His children through dreams and visions, if we will but have ears to hear and eyes to see. The language of the spirit is pictures, and the spirit can be touched most profoundly through the images that come to us from the Lord.

The rhema of God may come to us in the form of our conscience (Rom. 2:15) which either accuses or excuses us. And God will speak to us through His creation (Rom. 1:20), revealing truth to replace the error we have believed.

Elijah: From Faith to Fear to Faith

The story of Elijah's triumph over the prophets of Baal and subsequent depression is very familiar to us. But let's examine it once more and notice the *process* at work in Elijah's life which produced such profound "mood swings."

In I Kings 18:1-46, we read the story of Elijah's triumph over prophets of a false god because he heard God's voice and obeyed it. What a marvelous day that was! He called down fire from heaven, killed 350 false prophets, prayed earnestly and ended a three-year drought and outran a chariot for a distance of twenty miles. I would call that a successful day of ministry! He certainly was "God's man of the hour full of faith and power!" However, it is easy to forget that this was also a very draining day, spiritually, emotionally and physically. Therefore, he was a prime candidate for depression. It is good for us to realize that following our moments of greatest spiritual victory, we are most vulnerable to satan's attacks of fear, discouragement and depression, as well.

Satan never misses such an opportunity. In this case, he had a willing helper in the form of the wicked queen Jezebel. She sent word to Elijah, "I vow that I will have you killed within the next 24 hours." Here was rhema word from satan dropped into Elijah's mind. He had a choice. He could quiet his heart before the Lord and hear the Lord's response to the threat. Or he could do what he did do: receive the negative word, be filled with fear and run for his life. It is understandable. He had just been through a fierce spiritual battle. He was exhausted. He did not seem to have the strength to engage the enemy again. But satan fights dirty, attacking us when we are least prepared. So Elijah allowed the evil rhema to sink into his heart, and he began to incubate it.

His actions and words came under the control of the incubated rhema. In verses three and four we see him running into the wilderness, separating himself from those who would care for him, throwing himself down under a tree and wishing for death. "It is enough; now O Lord, take my life..." "I've had it. I'm no good and I just want to die." No matter how greatly we are used by God, it only takes a moment to receive an evil rhema and fall into depression.

But, praise God, we don't have to stay there! If we will receive it, our Father is waiting to restore us to faith. The first step in Elijah's healing was sleep. Sometimes, the most spiritual thing we can do is go to bed. If your mind and spirit are exhausted, don't stay up all night wrestling with the devil. Leave him in the Lord's hands and get some sleep. He will be much easier to defeat in the morning. The second step to restoration was to eat. There is a time when God calls us to fasting. Indeed, Elijah will go the next forty days without food. But right now, when his body and soul are weakened by spiritual battle, the Lord sends an angel with food and encouragement to eat and rebuild his strength.

Somewhat refreshed by the food and rest, Elijah now knows what he must do. "So he arose...and went...to the mountain of the Lord." At least his mind had cleared enough that he knew he had to hear from God. In verses eight through fourteen, his Father God gently and lovingly restores his divine perspective and renews his heart of faith. "What are you doing here, Elijah?" Of course God knew what he was doing there. But He wanted Elijah to express the fears that were strangling his spirit. "I have been very zealous for the Lord, the God of hosts; for the sons of Israel have forsaken Thy covenant, torn down Thine altars and killed Thy prophets with the sword. And I alone am left; and they seek my life, to take it away." Can you see the mixture of truth and error? Obviously, Elijah has been listening to the voice of the Liar. Before he is fully restored, he must accept the truth in place of these lies.

What did God say to Elijah in His still small voice? Did He rebuke him for his lack of faith? Did He condemn him for his weakness? Did He criticize him for listening to the enemy's voice? No, not at all. In verses 15 through 19 God responds to Elijah's fearful confession with the word, "Go..." God did not even mention the events of the last few days. Instead, He looked to the future and re-commissioned Elijah into ministry. He gave him authority to anoint kings. He instructed him to anoint another prophet to be with him and carry on his ministry. And finally, He spoke the truth to counter the lie Elijah had been incubating, "Yet I have left me seven thousand in Israel, all the knees which have not bowed unto Baal, and every mouth which hath not kissed him." Completely restored to a spirit of faith, Elijah went from the mountain of the Lord to carry on with the ministry God had called him to.

Summary

Jesus i the Counselor Who can destroy the debilitating fear which consumes us and ignite again the faith we need to live a life of victory. We must have a living experience with Him in which we take our fear before God in prayer. Then we must quiet ourselves to listen to His response and allow His words of truth to destroy the lie of the enemy. As a result, we will be free to praise and worship Him, rejoicing in His victory which we have received.

Response

Are there areas of fear in your life? To help you discern

them, write down all the endings to the question "What if...?" you have asked yourself recently. When you have laid all your fears before Jesus, quiet yourself in His presence and receive the mind of Christ on each situation. Record what He says and shows you. Unite faith with His words and enter into rest (Heb. 3).

Chapter Seven

From Guilt to Hope

Fear, guilt and anger are not only three of the great sins of the flesh, they are also three of the most physically destructive emotions we can entertain. They have been found to be contributing factors in a wide range of sickness and disease, including cancer. Now that we understand how the process of conception and incubation result finally in delivery, it is clear to us how the incubation of satan's destructive words and visions must have as its fruit sickness and death. However, our confidence is in the knowledge that the process also works for good, and the incubation of holy words and visions brings forth life, health and righteousness.

In the last chapter we learned how to overcome fear through hearing the voice of God. In this chapter we will examine the driving power of guilt and how it can be replaced by the drawing power of hope.

Just as there is true conviction of the Holy Spirit and false satanic condemnation, there is corresponding true guilt and false guilt. When we sin, God convicts us and we feel true guilt. This must be dealt with through confession and cleansing. However, when satan tries to immobilize with false guilt, no amount of repentance can set us free. False guilt must be dealt with in a totally different way.

I once read a statement by a mature Christian author to the effect that she would never act out of the motivation of guilt or rationality. Instead, she would only act on the impulse of love and rhema. That was a revolutionizing idea for me, because as I took stock of my own life, I discovered that I rarely did anything except out of guilt or because I reasoned that it was the right thing to do. I couldn't conceive of any other way to live. If guilt or reasoning did not motivate me, what would? And if the guilt that was motivating me wasn't right, what was wrong with it?

True Guilt

I knew that there was a place for true guilt in my life. When I sin, I "feel guilty" because I am guilty. How am I to handle this true guilt? How do I deal with the guilt of my sins and shortcomings? There are three essential revelation truths which must be firmly fixed in our minds and hearts in order to deal with true guilt:

1) *We must know our frame.*

David declared, "Just as a father has compassion on his children, So the Lord has compassion on those who fear Him. For He Himself knows our frame; He is mindful that we are but dust (Ps. 103:13,14)." Do I know that about myself? Am I mindful that I am but frail dust? Or do I have a vision of myself as something better than that? Do I see myself as strong as steel, supposedly able to withstand all the fiery darts of the enemy in my own strength. I must recognize that I will always be the weak one in our relationship and He will always be the strong one. When I think I am strong, I am at my weakest because I will trust in my own strength to be righteous and I must surely fail.

Not only am I weak, but I am a sinner. When Jesus was

hailed as "Good Teacher" (Mark 10:17), He replied, "Why do you call Me good? No one is good except God alone." Even Jesus, the perfect God-Man would not accept the title of "good" for Himself. Am I deluded into believing that *I* can become good? It is only because of His righteousness that we become holy and clean.

2) *We must know the righteousness that is by faith.*

We have "...hearts sprinkled clean from an evil conscience... (Heb. 10:22)." Only through faith in the blood of Jesus can our hearts be cleansed. Jesus Himself has become to us righteousness and sanctification, because we are in Him (I Cor. 1:30). We can never be free from the guilt of our sins if we do not accept the forgiveness and regeneration that comes to us by faith in the blood of Jesus.

We must see ourselves as God sees us, wearing a spotless robe of righteousness, clothed with Christ (Gal. 4:27), coming boldly before the throne of grace in time of need. This is the movie which must be continually played on the screen of our mind: I am only dust but I am fused to glory. I am clothed in a white robe of righteousness because of what Christ has done for me. By His grace and power, I can live righteous before my God.

3) *We must know the power that works within.*

The power to become righteous is not resident in my flesh, but it is available to me because of the One Who indwells me and fuses His strength to me. "I can do all things through Christ Who strengthens me (Phil. 4:13)." I can be strengthened with power through His Spirit in the inner man according to the power that works within me (Eph. 3:16,20).

When these truths become revelation knowledge to us by the power of the Holy Spirit, true guilt will no longer be a problem to us. When we sin, and we will, we will recognize our eternal weakness and bent toward sinning. Though we do not welcome or even accept our sinful condition, we are not surprised by it. We acknowledge our guilt, repenting earnestly and accept the righteousness that comes to us through faith in the blood of Jesus. Because God has forgiven us, we can forgive ourselves. We can pick ourselves up, even from the most shameful descent into sin, repent, receive forgiveness and go on, trusting in the power of the Spirit that works within us to keep us from falling again. We can receive the vision of truth from the Word of God that when He cleanses us from sin, we are truly clean and clothed in glorious white robes of righteousness.

False Guilt

True guilt comes as a result of the convicting power of the Holy Spirit, spot-lighting sin in our lives. It is specific, it urges my repentance, and it instructs me in positive actions to avoid missing the mark in the future.

Where then does false guilt come from? Ultimately, it finds its root in the accuser of the brethren. Unfortunately, it often finds its way into our minds through the well-intentioned words of our Christian pastors, elders, brothers and sisters. As we earnestly attempt to grow in our spiritual life, many voices call for our attention and demand our time, talents and money. The special speaker at church declares, "I pray six hours every day." The evangelist asserts, "I witness to everyone I meet and have led at least one person to the Lord every day for the last three years." The teacher exhorts, "You should read through the Bible every year." The pastor urges, "Whenever the church doors are open, you should be here. Also, you must attend a home cell group to be personally ministered to, and Bible School for your personal growth. And we really need Sunday School teachers, youth workers, janitors and volunteers in every department of the church." The family counselor admonishes, "Spend time every day with your family. Take your wife on a date once a week. Give your undivided attention to each child on a regular basis."

You start having chest pains from the stress of trying to meet the expectations of your church, and your doctor advises, "Get at least eight hours of sleep and exercise 45 minutes a day." On top of all these responsibilities, you must hold down a *very* good job in order to not only meet the needs of your own family but tithe to the church, and give to the building fund, the special speakers, special ministries, radio and television evangelists, the refugees, the North American Indians, the City Mission, world hunger and every other plea for money that crosses your doorstep! Where does it all end? How can you possibly live without guilt for having failed to do something important? No matter how good you are, you are never good enough to satisfy all the voices that clamor for your attention. Is there a way to be free?

Praise God, there is a way! When a multitude of voices scream for our attention, we must close our ears to them and listen only to the one Voice. We must discover what God's expectations are for our lives. We must know exactly what God wants us to be doing this year, this month, this week, this day and this hour. We do not live out of the expectations of other people, but only out of the commission of Christ to us personally.

Paul declared, "When they measure themselves by themselves, and compare themselves with themselves, they are *without understanding* (II Cor. 10:12b)." Comparing ourselves to each other can only result in confusion and frustration. We are never to compare ourselves with another person. We must only judge ourselves on the basis of what God has called us to do.

In order to determine God's expectations for me, I must discern His gifts and callings upon my life. If you aren't sure what gifts He has deposited within you, ask yourself the following questions: 1) What are the deep desires God has placed within my heart? What do I feel a burden for? 2) What are the areas and ministries in which I am effective? 3) In what areas does the Body of Christ confirm my effectiveness? If I am the only one who thinks I am a great teacher, I probably do not have the gift of teaching. However, if my students regularly express appreciation for the way the Lord has used my teaching to change their lives, there is little doubt about my gift and calling.

It is important to recognize that the gifts and callings of God upon your life may change from time to time. For example, when I first became a Christian, I felt a strong call to evangelism. I went from door-to-door, organized witnessing teams and used (or created) every opportunity to give the salvation message. As time went by, I gradually recognized an urge to shepherd those whom I had led to the Lord. The pastoral ministry became the burning desire of my heart and I served as youth pastor, associate pastor and finally senior pastor of a local fellowship. Eventually, I once again became aware of the stirring of the Spirit within my heart to change. Research and teaching became my greatest desire and the Body confirmed my gift in that dimension. At this time in my life, nothing gives me greater pleasure than studying the Word and sharing with others the truths revealed to me. I don't know if this call will continue for the rest of my life. Perhaps some time in the future the Lord will again stir up my heart to change. The important thing is that during this time I am free to be exactly what God wants me to be.

We all face the tendency to force others to fit into our mold. We must resist the temptation of "gift projection," in which we expect all Christians to feel the same burdens we feel, support the causes we support and exercise the same gifts we do, in the same way. This gift projection is the tool satan uses to bring false guilt and condemnation on so many Christians. We are part of a many-membered body, each individual having a unique and important ministry. If each member will do what God has called him to do and let everyone else do what God has called them to do, God's purposes will be accomplished on this earth.

Once we know what gifts God has placed within us, we still need revelation as to the way He wants that gift used. For example, many people in the Body have the gift of teaching, but it is expressed in different ways. Some are called to teach children and some adults. Some teach publicly in large groups, others privately in one-to-one encounters. Some teach verbally, others through writing books. You must seek the Lord for the specific task He has for you at this time in your life.

When the Lord tells you what His priorities are for your life, He will usually place a vision in your heart of the results of your accomplishing His goals for you. As you keep that vision before the eyes of your heart, hope will spring up within your spirit. This hope becomes the new motivation for action to replace the guilt under which we previously lived. Instead of being driven by guilt, we are now drawn by hope.

For instance, as a teacher, I have a hope of helping restore the fullness of the power of Jesus Christ to and through the Church. The vision of the Church glowing in full light and beauty has become a strong motivational force within me and I am no longer moved by guilt or duty.

Hope

Biblically speaking, hope is "a confident expectation of good." It is the mental frame of mind I have because of my faith in the presence and power of God. Although hope involves the mind, it is not merely wishful thinking.

Hope is part of the armor of God which we are to put on in order to stand against the attacks of the enemy. "Having put on the breastplate of faith and love, and as a helmet, the hope of salvation (I Thess. 5:8)." The helmet of hope is the protection God has provided for our head, our mind and our thoughts. As we look faithfully at the vision God has placed in our hearts, hope bubbles up and becomes the defense our minds need in spiritual warfare.

Hope is the by-product of being with Christ. Ephesians 2:12 says that to be separate from Christ is to be "without hope and without God in this world." When I forget to bring Christ into my considerations and calculations, I am without hope. When I do not see Christ in my life and circumstances, I have no hope. But when I am united to Christ, when I see Him working all things after the counsel of His will, when I see Him ruling and reigning in my life, hope is the stimulus that keeps me going.

What kept Jesus on the cross? In the midst of horrendous pain, when even His Father turned His back on Him, what motivation was strong enough to enable Him to fulfill the call of God upon His life? It was love that took Him to the cross, but it was hope that made Him stay. "For the joy set before Him [He] endured the cross, despising the shame (Heb. 12:2)." Jesus had a clear vision of what God planned to accomplish through His life and death. When every other motivation lost its power over Him, hope in the vision of joyfully bringing you and me with Him into glory guarded His mind and kept Him true to His call.

When we close our ears to the multitude of voices around us and open our inner ears to only the voice of Jesus, we will find ourselves moving forward with a singleness of mind and purpose which we have not experienced before. God's rhema will free us from the tyranny of the urgent as we act only in obedience to His leading. For the last several years, I have received a commission from God for the coming year on New Year's Eve. He has instructed me through rhema on where to focus my life and energies for the coming year. Instead of doing a half-hearted job on many projects, I am free to devote myself to doing an excellent job on one or two undertakings. Instead of haphazardly touching the surface of many areas of my life which need change and growth, I am able to concentrate without guilt on the one specific area God wants to work on that year. I have found that by being obedient to His direction, major changes have been made in my spiritual life which in turn affect every area of my life.

But what about all the things we turn our back on and leave undone? The accuser will do his best to bring worry and guilt back upon us regarding those things. When he tries to ensnare you with these thoughts, remind him that you are no longer a slave to his tricks. No longer are you a puppet on his string, jerked back and forth by every crying need. You are about your Father's business. You are doing what God designed you to do and that is all you can be concerned about.

As Jesus hung on the cross He said, "It is finished." There were still many souls to be saved. There were still many sick to be healed, oppressed to be delivered and hungry to be fed. How could He possibly think anything was finished? Only because Jesus knew why God had sent Him to earth could He leave in peace. The work God had given Him to do was done.

Summary

Guilt is a powerful motivating force in many people's lives. If we are to break free, we must learn to distinguish between true and false guilt and deal with each properly. True guilt is a result of the conviction of the Holy Spirit. Our only response must be to agree with the Lord, repent of our sin, receive the righteousness of God through faith and appropriate His power to overcome in the future.

False guilt comes as a result of allowing the accuser to gain a foothold in our minds. Freedom from such guilt comes as we reject the demands of the enemy and listen only to the voice of Jesus. He will give us focus, direction and vision for our lives.

From this vision, hope will spring up within, guarding our minds from future attacks of satan.

Response

Determine in your heart that you will no longer be a slave to the overwhelming demands that are made on your life, your time, your talents and your money. Instead, ask the Lord what He wants your current focus to be, what He wants you to be doing and what He does not want you to be doing. Examine your heart to see if there are any areas of your life in which you do not have a "confident expectation of good." If there are, take them to Jesus and record the rhema and vision He gives, so that you are no longer "without hope and without Christ."

Chapter Eight

From Anger to Love

Is there anyone in your life who causes your blood pressure to go up, just by hearing their name? Is there someone who can start your stomach churning with anger or resentment, just by walking into the room? Are there events in your past that you rehearse over and over again in your mind, keeping your anger and bitterness alive? When you hear the words "anger" and "forgive," is there any name that comes immediately to your mind?

How easy it is to fall into the life-style of incubating anger and unforgiveness! When someone hurts us, or deprives us of our rights, or treats us unfairly, it is easy to become obsessed with the negative emotions that rise up within us. But what is the effect on us when we are angry? Our muscles contract, we become tense in every part of our bodies, we are vulnerable to pain and sickness, and our spirits are strangled, prevented from drawing deeply upon the Spirit of Life. We become a slave not only to the emotions which control us, but to the one with whom we are angry as well. Because we perceive their actions as the cause of our condition, we are in bondage to them.

Anger and unforgiveness are among the most common needs which drive people to medical doctors and professional counselors. Is it possible for us to find release and healing from these crippling emotions at the feet of our Counselor Jesus? Not only is it possible, it is His deep desire to minister the Spirit of Love to you that can set you free — more free than you have ever been in your life.

Understanding Anger

Anger is not a sin. The Bible does not command us not to be angry. Rather, it exhorts, "Be angry, and sin not... (Eph. 44:26)." The anger is not the problem. Our response to the anger we feel is the problem. How we deal with our anger determines whether we sin or have victory.

If anger is not a sin, what is it? Bill Gothard has given the following definition: "Anger is an inner alarm system revealing personal rights which we have either not given to God, or have taken back from Him." Let's examine this definition carefully.

"Anger is an inner alarm system..." Anger lets us know there is a problem within us. It warns us that the security system of our spirits has been breached in some way. It alerts us to the need to shore up our defenses against sin in some area of our lives. The first response must be to find out what triggered the alarm, then neutralize the enemy which is attempting to steal our peace.

"Anger...reveals personal rights which we have either not given to God, or have taken back from Him." We have been born with certain rights. Our constitution includes among these "inalienable rights" life, liberty and the pursuit of happiness. As Christians, we might include other "rights" which have been given to us as children of God — perhaps the right to joy, health, prosperity, answered prayers, whatever your particular doctrine defines as the rights of the covenant of salvation. We live in a society that is obsessed with protecting its rights and demanding more. Our court system is over-whelmed with individuals and groups suing other individuals and groups for depriving them of what they perceive to be their rights. Even the Church has been infected with the spirit which demands its due, even from God. We hear that God has promised us something in the Word, and we must simply claim it as our rightful inheritance. After all, it is our right!

How far this is from the example of our Lord. In Philippians 2:5-8 we see a totally different approach to life.

> "Have this attitude in yourselves which was also in Christ Jesus, who, although He existed in the form of God, did not regard equality with God a thing to be grasped, but emptied Himself, taking the form of a bond-servant, and being made in the likeness of men, And being found in appearance as a man, He humbled Himself by becoming obedient to the point of death, even death on a cross."

Jesus had a right to be worshipped as God because He was God! Jesus had a right to be treated with respect for He was the Lord of the Universe. He had a right to exercise all power and authority over every created thing, because He was the Creator. He had a right to life, because He is the Giver of Life. He had a right to a fair trial, since He is the Righteous Judge. He had a right to receive justice, for He is Just.

Yet how did He view His rights? He "did not regard [them] a thing to be grasped." He did not demand His rights but instead emptied Himself of every one. Rather than clenching His hands to hang on to His rights, He opened His hands and let them be nailed to a cross.

"Have this attitude in yourselves which was also in Christ Jesus." God wants us to yield all our personal rights and possessions, every blessing that we think we deserve, to Him, and let Him decide if and when He will return them to us. We may believe we have a "right" to a good reputation. God says,

"Give your reputation to me." We think we have a right to plan our time and live under an orderly schedule. God says, "Let me be the Lord of your time." We believe we have a right to personal dignity. God says, "Trust yourself to Me." Herein is lordship. Are we willing to give God everything, our children, our marriage, our future, our health, friends, business, money, sexual life? Do we really believe that He loves us and is willing and able to work all things out for our good? Can we totally trust Him to take care of everything that is important to us without placing conditions or offering suggestions about how He should handle it?

If we have emptied ourselves of everything, as Christ did, there will be no place for anger. We become angry when we believe that one of our rights has been violated. Think about it for a moment. What was the last thing you became angry about? Was it unfair treatment at work? Why did that make you angry? Because you have a *right* to be treated fairly and with dignity. Why do you become angry when your children misbehave? Because you have a *right* to respect and obedience and a peaceful home and a good reputation as a parent. Why do you become angry when your possessions are damaged? Because they belong to you, you bought them with money you worked hard to earn, they are your responsibility, and you have a right to enjoy them.

Therefore, anger becomes a warning system that alerts us to any rights or possessions we have either not entrusted to the Lord's care, or have taken back from Him. If we sense anger welling up within us, our response should be to examine our hearts, under the illumination of the Spirit, to determine what "right" has been violated. When we give that right back to Him, our anger will end.

To remain free of anger, we must: 1) Yield the right to God (Phil. 2:5-8). 2) Realize that God will test His rights (Gen. 22:1-14). Usually a time of consecration is followed by a time of testing, not to humble us through our failures but to demonstrate the marvelous power we have released by giving the Lord free reign in our lives. 3) Respond to the loss of rights with a godly attitude. We do not become doormats with no character who welcome every loss or put down. We do not become passive masochists. We become worshipers, glorying in the power of God to handle all that we cannot, and work it for our good. "The Lord giveth, the Lord taketh away, Blessed be the name of the Lord (Job 1:21b)."

Once again, we must realize that legalistic adherence to this formula will never produce life, only death. If we, by our own efforts, force ourselves to crush our anger and ritualistically turn our rights back over to the Lord, we will become spirit-less, character-less, religious robots. That is not what God wants from us. He wants us joyful, exuberant, bubbling with life and vitality! What He wants only comes through encounter with Christ.

The Emmaus road experience is the only path to true freedom. Let's adjust our "formula" for healing once again. When we feel anger rising within us, we must 1) Immediately turn to Jesus and tell Him how we feel (Lk. 24:13-24). For me, journaling is the most effective means of doing so. Remember, we want to talk it over with Jesus, not our neighbor. We can carry on a conversation with another person in which we each express our angers and frustrations and accomplish nothing except greater anger and frustration. Only if someone brings in the wisdom of Christ is it beneficial to share your negative emotions with another. 2) After we have emptied our hearts of all the destructive feelings, we must quiet ourselves and listen to the Lord's response (Lk. 24:25-30). Sometimes He will illumine Scripture to our hearts. Sometimes He will speak through a brother. Sometimes He will speak directly through journaling. He will show us the gift He wants to give us through the bad experience. Perhaps we will grow in character, or poise, or godliness, or faith, or perseverance because of what happened, if we allow the Lord to use it for our good. He does not condone the sinful behavior which caused us pain, but He does promise that through it, we can become more like Him. 3) We must unite His words with faith and take on Christ's reaction (Lk. 24:31-35). Complete healing and forgiveness comes only when we receive the working of God in the pain and accept the gift He wants to give us through it.

Understanding Love

I have noticed that some people are more prone to anger than others. Some people seem to find it quite easy to look with compassion and forgiveness upon those who wound them. For them, seeing God at work even in painful situations and receiving the gift from them is no problem. For others, anger never seems far from the surface and is likely to break out at the slightest provocation. People like us (yes, I must number myself among this group) often have a hard time accepting that the guilty person who wronged us deserves to be forgiven.

Of course, because I was a Christian, my anger was justified. It wasn't really anger, it was "righteous indignation" over the sins of others! When I recognized error in another's theology, the wrath of God arose within me to vindicate truth. When a so-called brother stepped from the narrow path of righteousness and brought shame on the name of Christ through sin, holy indignation moved me to rebuke and correct the sinner. At least that's the way I perceived it. I thought truth, knowledge of right and wrong, was the center of Christianity. I believed that doctrinal purity and unswerving adherence to a strict moral code were the proofs of Christianity and the basis of my fellowship with others.

Thankfully, the Lord had mercy on me (and my wife, and my children, and my church!) and showed me a better way to live. He showed me from scripture that God is both Light and

Love. Both words reveal one aspect of His character. But what do these words mean? How is the character of Light revealed in God, and how does He demonstrate Love? Consider the following chart:

	God Is:	
Light	and	**Love**
Rightness		Love
Judgement		Forgiveness
Challenge		Reconciliation
Confrontation		Healing
Division		Unity
Hatred of Sin		Love of Sinner
Condemnation		Comfort
Justice		Mercy
Infinite Precision		Matchless Grace

The character traits and activities of both columns are found in God. My life centered primarily around column one. I entered every situation prepared to judge the rightness of the people and theology, challenge and confront anything I found to be out of line, separate myself from anything and anyone questionable, insist on infinite precision to the Law and demand justice for all transgressors. This attitude had been fed by all the churches I had ever attended, as well as the teaching of my Christian college professors. I believed it was godly. And, to a certain extent, it was. God exhibits all those same traits. However, my life lacked the balancing character of the "Love" column.

The Lord took me to Micah 6:8: "He has showed thee, O man, what is good; and what does the Lord require of thee but to do justice and to love mercy and to walk humbly with thy God?" God *loves* to show mercy, but only *does* justice because righteousness demands it. I was just the opposite: I loved justice and only did mercy if I felt it was deserved. I loved what

God did, and did what God loved. No wonder my life was so unfulfilling.

Although God is Light which must stand against darkness, His greatest joy is to show Love. Although sin must be challenged, He offers reconciliation to Him and to one another. To Him, unity is more important than doctrinal purity. For someone like me, who had always aspired to truth above all else, it was a life-changing revelation to discover that Truth is a Person, and that Person is Love.

John wrote his gospel that those who read might believe and have eternal life (John 20:31). He wrote his first epistle to those "who believe in the name of the Son of God, in order that you may know that you have eternal life (I John 5:13)." This letter offers proofs of salvation by which we may judge ourselves and others. They are summarized in I John 3:23, "And this is His commandment, that we believe in the name of His Son Jesus Christ, and love one another, just as He commanded us." Two simple tests: Who is Jesus? and Love one another. The only doctrinal truth that must be intact is that Jesus Christ is the eternal Son of God. All other theological theories and beliefs are not legitimate cause for division. If you have accepted the cleansing work of Jesus on the cross, you are my brother, and I must love you.

Recognizing and accepting God's evaluation of the imbalance in my life was only the first step to change. Although I was commanded to love, the power was not resident in my flesh to do so. I had to repent of my sin (even an over-emphasis on holiness can be sin if you miss the mark of perfect, agape love), turn away from my old ways, receive His forgiveness, and accept His grace and power to change. He gave me an assignment so that I was working in cooperation with the Spirit within. First, I read the Gospels through several times, looking especially at the way Jesus loved people. I also studied the Psalms, learning how to process my emotions before God where they could be healed and not damage anyone else. Finally, I re-read my journal, observing how He loved me. As my mind and spirit became focused on the amazing love which permeates every word and every act Jesus ever did, the Holy Spirit was able to re-shape my heart to be more like His. My judgmental, fractured heart was healed and I became an instrument of reconciliation and healing in His hand. What freedom! What joy!

Summary

Anger is an indication that there are areas of our life which we have not completely placed under the lordship of Jesus Christ. When we sense anger rising within us, we must come before the Lord, listen to His voice and act in obedience to it. We must learn to process all our emotions before God, giving Him the opportunity to reveal Himself at work in our lives.

God is Love and He is Light. He loves to show mercy and compassion on His children. Every word He speaks and every deed He does is bathed in non-performance-oriented love. Because He is also righteous, He requires holiness and justice, but all of His judgments are tempered with mercy.

As we abide in His presence, spend time communing with Him, watch Him at work in the spiritual world, always working all things out for our good, our hearts will be molded into His likeness. We will begin to love mercy. We will look on every situation as an opportunity to show compassion and express to someone the overwhelming love that fills our hearts.

Response

Is there anyone against whom you are harboring anger? Is there someone who hurt you so deeply that you have been unable to forgive them? Has the Lord been speaking to your heart about rights which you have not yielded to Him? Express whatever is on your heart to the Lord, then give Him a chance to respond. Perhaps He will lead you into an inner healing

Chapter Nine

From Inferiority to Identify

Do you ever feel like the demands upon you are just too great and you simply haven't the strength to meet them? Do the responsibilities you face threaten to overwhelm you and send you plunging into despair? As you look at the people around you who are facing similar challenges, do they seem better equipped and more capable than you? Do you exhaust yourself trying to accomplish all that is expected of you each day without ever quite reaching the bottom of the pile? Have you ever felt inadequate, insecure, or inferior?

I'm sure you have struggled with such feelings from time to time. Maybe for you it's just an occasional problem. Or perhaps it is such a pervasive problem that it cripples you emotionally, preventing you from even making the attempt to achieve the desires of your heart. Does Jesus care when we are in the grips of these devastating emotions? Is He willing and able to lift us from their clinging grasp and give us the security and sense of wholeness and adequacy we so desperately need? Praise His name, He is not only willing to do so, He has been praying that you would find your identity in Him since He walked upon this earth as a man. Even on the night before He

died, though He knew He was facing torture both in the flesh
and the spirit, you were on His heart and He prayed earnestly
that you would accept your unity with Him which alone can
set you from inadequacy and inferiority (Jn. 17:21,23).

The Causes of Inferiority

You know how inferiority and self-rejection feel. You have
held yourself up in comparison to others and found yourself
lacking. You have tried to cover your inadequacies by giving
over-attention to your clothes or awkwardly trying to hide
those things about yourself which you cannot accept. You
have experienced the floating bitterness which can be expressed
toward almost anyone but is really directed toward yourself
and God, Who made you the way you are. Perhaps you have
over-compensated for your weaknesses with perfectionism.
Probably your tongue has been silenced and your brain frozen
in shyness by the belief that since you can't accept yourself, no
one else would want to know you either.

Where do such destructive feelings and actions come from?
Of course, ultimately they are the works of satan in our lives.
But how is he able to so completely deceive us that we turn
against ourselves? Again, the answer is the same as we have
seen in the other sin areas we have considered. When we take
our eyes away from Jesus and fix them on ourselves, others or
satan's hateful delusions, we will always have an inappropriate
self image. Only as we fix our eyes on Jesus can we clearly see
ourselves.

Cause #1: Wrong Comparisons:

One of the major causes of an inaccurate self-image is
comparing ourselves with others. "For when they measure
themselves by themselves, and compare themselves with
themselves, they are without understanding (II Cor. 10:12b)."
We may compare our physical appearance — height, weight,
hair, skin, and perceived conformity to a mythical ideal. We

may compare our spirituality — amount of time spent in prayer, Bible verses memorized, and people won to the Lord. Or we might compare our gifts — academic ability, musical talent, or any of the multitude of ways in which God gifts us.

Comparing myself with others will always result in a wrong attitude. If I compare myself only with those over whom I feel I excel, I will develop an attitude of superiority. If I compare myself with those whom I feel are better than me in any particular way, I feel inferior. How then can I judge myself? If I am not to compare myself to others, how will I know if I am performing adequately and being successful? In a society which has no absolute standards, we have nothing to compare ourselves to except each other and we have indeed become "without understanding." Even in school, we are graded not according to our own ability but in comparison to the others in the class. No wonder school has such a destructive effect on so many children.

How then shall we know when we have succeeded? "For not he who commends himself is approved, but whom the Lord commends (II Cor. 10:18)." Positive identity comes when we compare ourselves to the Lord's expectations for our lives. He created each of us with unique physical character-istics, intellectual abilities and spiritual gifts. He has special tasks for each of us to do during our lives and He has fashioned us to be perfectly suited to accomplish them. He does not judge us on the basis of the gifts He has given to anyone but us. "To whom much is given, much is required (Luke 12:48)." If we allow Him to show us ourselves exactly as He sees us, we will be amazed and echo the words of the Psalmist, "I will give thanks to Thee, for I am fearfully and wonderfully made; Wonderful are Thy works, and my soul knows it very well (Ps. 139:14)."

The Lord judges us on the basis of His perfect knowledge of us. Remember the parable of the talents (Matt. 25:14-30). The master gave to each of the servants on the basis of his ability. The first two servants, who had received five and two talents respectively, through the wise use of the talents returned five and two more. To the first servant, who had earned five more, the master said, "Well done, good and faithful slave; you are faithful with a few things, I will put you in charge of many things; enter into the joy of your master." The second servant only increased the master's wealth by two talents. How did the master respond? Did he ask why he had not also earned five talents, as had the other slave? Did he criticize him for not performing as well as another? Not at all. Instead, he spoke the very same words of blessing to the one who earned two as to the one who earned five: "Well done, good and faithful slave, you were faithful with a few things, I will put you in charge of many things; enter into the joy of your master." The Lord knows our abilities and expects nothing more nor less than our very best.

What about the areas of our life that are clear weaknesses? How can we have a positive self-image in the face of our inabilities and defects? "He has said to me, 'My grace is sufficient for you, for power is perfected in weakness.' Most gladly, therefore, I will rather boast about my weaknesses, that the power of Christ may dwell in me. Therefore I am well content with weaknesses...for when I am weak, then I am strong (II Cor. 12:9,10)." When we offer our weaknesses to Christ to be filled with His strength, our areas of weakness become our areas of greatest strength. There is no need for shame or embarrassment or dissatisfaction with our inabilities, because they are the very vehicle through which Christ can be most gloriously manifested in our lives. "But God has chosen the foolish things of the world to shame the wise, and God has chosen the weak things of the world to bring to shame the things which are strong...that no man should boast before God...that, just as it is written, 'Let him who boasts, boast in the Lord' (I Cor. 1:27,29,31)."

When I was in school, I was not a very eager student. I hated English, spelling, grammar, reading, writing and public speaking. I was never a scholar in these areas, and to this day they are among my areas of greatest weakness. Yet God has chosen to use me, with my poor grammar and terrible spelling, to give a message to the Church through the written word. I do not take pride in my weakness, nor can I take pride in what is accomplished through me, because it is obviously the working of Christ which makes it possible.

What about my areas of strength? How shall I view them? First, I am expected to use all of my abilities to their fullest. As I exercise my talents in the service of the Lord, they are stretched and increased. Just as the servant in the parable mentioned above received five talents, used them to develop five more and as a result was given an additional one, so we can use our talents to develop more and increase our giftedness. Second, we are to use our strengths to bless those who are weak. Rather than becoming boastful and lording over those who do not have the same gifts as we, we must yield our gifts to them to cover their weaknesses and give them strength.

This attitude should pervade every area of our lives, from home and family to church and business. For example, most husbands and wives are very different. That's why they were attracted to one another in the first place. Each saw within the other gifts and abilities which they did not have in their own lives and it drew them together. Unfortunately, after the honeymoon, a subtle change often takes place. Rather than honoring the strengths of our partner, we condemn their weaknesses. Rather than supporting each other with our strengths, we begin to compete against each other for respect and affirmation. God wants those attitudes of competition and criticism to change. He has placed us together that our united strengths will overcome our united weaknesses and as a single entity, in His strength, we will be able to handle anything.

Cause #2: Not Understanding or Appropriating Biblical Principles

You were created in the image of almighty God. You are so important to Him that He was willing to allow His only Son to die a terrible death in order to bring you back into fellowship with Him. The very God, Creator of the universe, knows you and calls you by name. The Bible has much to say on the dignity of man and why He wants you to have a positive self-image. Many good books have been written on the subject and I recommend that everyone struggling with inferiority read at least one in order to build a theological and philosophical foundation for self-esteem. *You're Someone Special* by Bruce Narramore and *His Image, My Image* by Josh McDowell are especially helpful.

I will not spend a lot of time covering material which can be found elsewhere. I only want to add one spiritual concept which is often over-looked. Genesis chapters 2 and 3 clearly teach that we were created to be kings and queens and to rule. God designed us to be His Regents upon this earth, to reign out of a position of submission to His supreme authority. Deep within us is a hunger to be honored as the royalty which we are. As we are joined in covenant to God through salvation, we are once again restored to our position as kings and priests and this driving appetite for esteem is satisfied. When we attempt to attain honor or power or position through any means besides submission to the King of Kings, we are doomed to sin and failure.

This truth, as well as those found in the recommended books, cannot heal you or deliver you from deep inferiority. Only a revelation of the Spirit to your heart as you meet Jesus face-to-face can heal your soul. These concepts provide a foundation of truth from which the Lord can draw out rhema to meet your particular need. Only an encounter with the living God can give you life.

One cannot be whole by living in *principles* of truth, no matter how good these principles are. The religious people of Jesus' day "searched the scriptures, because they thought that in *them* they would have eternal life." Jesus told them that "It is these that bear witness of Me, and you are unwilling to come to Me, that you may have life (Jn. 5:39,40)." Eternal life is knowing God, being totally intimate with Him (Jn. 17:3). It is experiencing the same reality of inner union with God that Jesus had.

Cause #3: Living on the Surface

Finally, a good self-image occurs whenever we experience our inner union with Jesus Christ. The Bible says, "to live is Christ," and that "Christ is my life." Over and over again in the New Testament we find this beautiful union spoken of. "I have been crucified with Christ; and it is no longer I who live, but Christ lives in me; and the life which I now live in the flesh I live by faith in the Son of God... (Gal. 2:20)." It is the experience of inner union that heals my inferiority, insecurity and sense of inadequacy and allows me to experience my identity with Christ.

It is so easy to lose sight of that union and return to living on the surface of my life. I feel hollow within, and because the "I" is no longer the "Christ-I" but myself, I face the issues of life alone. My self-image is destroyed; I feel fractured, torn apart, stretched out.

Probably there are times when we all feel this way. There are days when I enter my office in the morning to find it piled high with mail to answer, calls to return, classes to prepare, and books to write. Because I enjoy working, I may dig right in, confident that I can handle it all. But as the day wears on, other phone calls interrupt, people drop in who need to talk, my staff needs input, and my frustration begins to rise. By noon it becomes clear that I *can't* handle it and the work won't be finished that day. If I continue the day as I have begun it, trusting in my own ability, the afternoon will be a disaster. I will be tense and irritable, short-tempered and venting my own sense of inadequacy on everyone who ventures near me. At the end of the day, very little of what I planned to do will be done and I will have lost every trace of the peace that comes from living in unity with Christ.

But the day doesn't have to go that way. From the moment I awaken in the morning, I can entrust myself and my activities to the guidance of the Spirit. When I enter my office and see the abundance of tasks calling for my time and attention, I can quiet myself before the Lord, asking Him what *He* wants me to do that day. I can confess once more that I no longer live but Christ is now my life. I can confidently trust Him to face the issues of my life and move through me to make the right decisions. He will show me where to begin and give His grace that I may be productive in accomplishing what is required of me. Sometimes He will direct me to something that wasn't even on my list of priorities. But if I am willing to trust His wisdom, I can go through the day in peace, knowing that I am doing the Lord's will in the Lord's strength, and He will take care of the consequences. Then when interruptions come, I can welcome them as from the Lord. As long as I abide in Him, there will be peace and joy not only in my own heart, but in the lives of those I touch as I become a minister of Christ to them.

My unity with Christ is an eternal fact if I am born again. Nothing can separate me from Him. It is not that I am actually living apart from Him; it is only my perception which is faulty. Therefore, when I recognize that I have begun to operate out of a false independence, I do not waste time berating myself but quickly repent and return to the truth in my heart. It is necessary that we all know the best ways to help us move from surface illusions to true inner reality. For myself, heartfelt praise, worship and journaling are the most effective avenues. For some, it may be reading the Word or sitting beside a bubbling brook or snuggled by an open fire or doing an automatic activity. Discover the things you can do which make you aware of the Lord's presence within you and use them whenever you need to return to living out of that union.

Summary

Inferiority is a problem that pervades our society. There are many causes of this sense of not quite measuring up: wrongly comparing ourselves to other people, not knowing or applying some basic biblical truths about self-esteem, and living without an awareness of my unity with Christ. The development of an accurate self-image comes out of time spent in the Lord's presence. He will teach us about ourselves, helping us to recognize and use our strengths to serve Him and others, and offer our weaknesses to Him to be filled that He might be glorified. He will take the truths of Scripture and make them revelation knowledge which can transform our hearts. And He will gently lead us into an ever more consistent life of abiding in the knowledge of our union with Him.

Response

How big a problem is inferiority, insecurity and inadequacy in your life? As you read through the chapter, did the Spirit show you the contributing factors to your poor self-image? If not, ask Him to show you now. Then quiet yourself and receive the revelation which He wants to give you that can heal your aching heart.

Chapter Ten

From Depression to Joy

I am sure you know what it is like: the sadness, hopelessness, anxiety, and hostility, the "weeps," the loss of appetite (or uncontrolled gorging), the apathy and erratic sleep behavior. What can have such overwhelming control over our lives? We call it depression, and I dare say that every single person has faced it at some point in his life. In America, one out of eight people will be so crippled by its heaviness that they will seek profession help. An even greater percentage will trudge wearily through life, accepting the blackness that clouds their heart as normal and inescapable.

Is there a way out of this web of despair? Is it possible to *do* something which can hasten a return of the sunlight in our souls? Is there a reason for hope? I offer as evidence my own testimony of freedom after ten years' struggle with depression that, yes, there is a way of escape.

Depression Defined

Depression may be defined as "giving in to the pressures of life while letting go of our faith in God." Depression is the direct result of listening to the wrong voices and focusing on the wrong vision. When I listen to the lies of the accuser and stop my ears to the comfort and wisdom of the spirit of God, I have started down the road of depression. When I fix my eyes on the circumstances around me, how they are affecting me and how I will attempt to handle them, while ignoring the promises and purposes of God in my life, I have set my face toward the darkness of despondency.

There are a few people who very rarely feel the cold touch of depression. Most people experience mild or even serious depression occasionally throughout their lives. Others constantly live under the black cloud of severe depression that swallows up every joy, leaving only an empty void in its place. But regardless of the level of depression you face, "the Lord is near to the brokenhearted and saves those who are crushed in spirit (Ps. 34:18)." The Lord has promised a way out for you!

Catalysts and Causes of Depression

As I indicated earlier, I struggled against the effects of depression in my own Christian life for ten years. I earnestly sought the Lord for wisdom about this crippling force and deliverance from it. I believe that He answered my prayers through the chart shown on the following page.

Around the outside you will see some of the physical and emotional manifestations of depression. These will vary from person to person, depending on individual personality. However, many of the characteristics listed will be seen in the life of the depressed person.

The next circle lists some of the most common surface causes of depression, including: life's trying circumstances, unconfessed sin, religiosity, sickness or physical malfunction, poor care of the body and lack of personal discipline. Often, if we are asked why we are feeling depressed, we will point to one of these: "My life is so hard. I think I'm coming down with the flu. I didn't get enough sleep last night." It appears that our unhappiness and depression spring from these sources.

However, I would like to suggest that these are not *causes* but merely *catalysts* which precipitate the manifestation of depression. In other words, it is not the difficulty which is facing me that is causing me to be depressed. If that were true, everyone in the same circumstances would respond in the same way. This is simply not true. While many people do indeed sink into depression while in the midst of stressful events, other people are able to respond positively and rise above their trials to new levels of faith and character. Therefore, we must look deeper to find the true source of the depressive response.

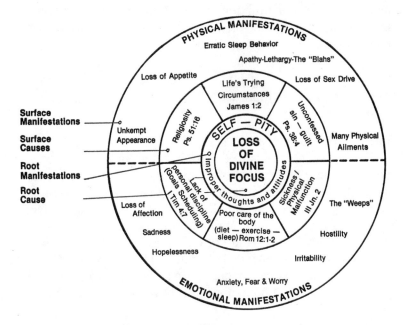

Moving one step closer to the core of the circle, underlying the negative apparent causes of depression, there is a layer called "self-pity." This, I believe, is the underlying root manifestation for the majority of depression people face. "Poor me, my life is so miserable. Poor me, I don't feel well. Poor me, I can't seem to get control of my life. Poor, me, life is so unfair." Wrong thoughts and attitudes permeate our mind and spirit so that when sickness, trials or uncontrollable circumstances enter our lives, they immediately plunge us into the dark abyss.

But how do we become so full of self-pity? Very simply, by losing our divine focus. Instead of focusing on God and His purposes, we focus on ourselves and the lying words of satan. Rather than fixing our eyes on Jesus, we look only at the unhappiness of our situation. Rather then quieting our hearts to hear the still small voice of the Spirit within, we thrash about in surface reaction. The cure, then, to most of the depression we face is in hearing the voice of God and seeing the vision of God. But let us examine each of the surface causes or catalysts more carefully to see how this principle applies to each.

Life's Trying Circumstances

Not everyone reacts to the trials of life in the same way. Some see only the pressure, feel only the pain, and hear only the destroyer's voice. These respond with anger, bitterness and depression. Others respond as Paul and James commanded: "Consider it all *joy*, my brethren, when you encounter various trials... (James 1:2)." "And not only this, but we also *exult* in our tribulations, knowing that tribulation brings about perseverance, and perseverance, proven character, and proven character hope, and hope does not disappoint... (Rom. 5:3-5, emphasis added)."

How can we possibly be expected to not only accept trials without complaint, but actually leap for joy when tribulation and sorrow are upon us? There is only one way. We must be convinced that the "Most High is the ruler over the realm of mankind" and that He always "causes all things to work together for [our] good... (Rom. 8:28)." We must have not only a theological conviction of His great love for man, but an experiential knowledge of His tender mercy toward us as individuals. We must hear His voice promising that through this tragedy, He will bring good.

It is easy for us to believe that holy, just men can be used by God to achieve His purposes. After all, they seek His will and move in obedience to it. It is more difficult to accept that the hateful, jealous acts of spiteful men can have any place in the plan of God for our lives. Surely wicked men acting out of their selfish initiative are beyond the redemptive power of the Lord. Yet it is definitely not so.

God promised Joseph that he would rule over his entire family, even his parents. But soon afterward he was sold into slavery while on a errand for his father, thrown into prison for not succumbing to immorality, and forgotten by those whom he helped. It must have been hard for Joseph to believe that God's hand was upon him. There must have been times on that auction block and in that dark prison cell when he was tempted to doubt God's promise to him and give in to anger and depression. But the Bible indicates that he kept his heart pure. He didn't curl into a ball in the corner, nursing his self-pity with a rehearsal of the injustices heaped upon him, though surely if anyone had a right, it was he. Nor did he lash out in anger at the ones who held him under their control. Always his spirit was so pure that he gained favor even among his captors and owners. Always he conducted himself with such dignity that he was given authority over his peers. How was he able to withstand such hardship and tribulation? Because always before the eyes of his heart was the vision God had given him in his youth, strengthening his faith and giving him hope. So firmly was that vision planted in his heart that he was able to receive those who wronged him with love and forgiveness, affirming that though they meant evil against him, God meant it for good (Gen. 50).

The apostle Paul experienced great suffering during his Christian life. He was stoned, beaten, imprisoned, and mocked. He was "afflicted in every way, but not crushed; perplexed, but not despairing; persecuted, but not forsaken; struck down, but not destroyed (II Cor. 4:8,9)." Why was he able to rise above all of these trials and write, even from a prison cell, "Rejoice in the Lord always, and again I say, Rejoice!" Why did he not despair? Because he knew in his heart that all that was happening to him was for a purpose, that all his suffering was having a positive result: "For all things are for your sakes, that the grace which is spreading to more and more people may cause the giving of thanks to abound to the glory of God (II Cor. 4:15)." The vision God had given him was to be a messenger of the good news of Christ to the Gentiles. That was his only goal in life, and the trials that came upon him were instruments in accomplishing that goal. God was using his suffering to work grace into the lives of others. "So momentary, light affliction is producing for us an eternal weight of glory far beyond all comparison, while we look not at the things which are seen, but at the things which are not seen; for the things which are seen are temporal, but the things which are not seen are eternal (II Cor. 4:17,18)." Compared with the wondrous joy of spending eternity with those whom he had won to Christ, the suffering he experienced seemed but momentary and light. When he sat in that dirty prison, wounded and bleeding from the beating he had received, he did not even think about the material, physical world and his own pain. Rather, he kept his gaze fixed on the eternal truth which is not seen with earthly eyes but only through a revelation of the Spirit, the eternal salvation of souls.

A number of years ago, I was led by the Lord to resign from my position as pastor of a local fellowship. Because I had a wife and two small children to support, my first thought was to find a job. I wasn't too worried about my chances, even though it was a time of great unemployment, because I enjoy physical labor and am willing to do anything to earn an honest living. My first thought was to cut and sell firewood. I had grown up on a farm and enjoyed being back in the woods again. For a few weeks, everything went well and the money was good. Then, suddenly, my back could no longer handle the strain. I had a weakness in my back since a childhood accident, but with care I was always able to manage. The constant strain of chopping and lifting, however, was more than it could bear.

Thank God I had learned to journal and was able to turn to Him for wisdom during this difficult time. I expressed my frustration at not being able to earn a living through the strength of my right arm. I told Him of my concerns about how I would take of my family. I pleaded with Him to heal my back that I could continue working. But He replied, "Mark, you have never been able to trust me for finances. You have always trusted in your own labor and industry to supply your need. I want you to learn that I am your Source and I can be depended upon, even when your efforts are futile. I don't want you chopping wood or working in a factory. I have called you to teach My people. I don't want you seeking a paying job anywhere right now. I want you to volunteer your services to a particular ministry. Trust me to take care of the finances."

I wish I could say that I immediately obeyed the word of the Lord. Unfortunately, He was right. I didn't trust Him for money. It didn't seem right to me that a man should not work to support his family if he is able. So, the Lord saw to it that I was unable. He did not heal my back and the continued pain and stress became unbearable. All the time He kept repeating the same message in my journal. Finally, I accepted Him at His word, left the job hunting and volunteered at the church He had specified. I guess I hoped that once He saw my obedience, He would consider that I had learned my lesson in faith and He would give me a paying job. I was wrong. For eight months I was unemployed. I had no home, no car and no income, for everything had been owned by my previous church. Every week I would ask the Lord if I couldn't find paying employment, and every week He said, "Wait and trust in Me." Slowly I began to recognize His power at work for me. He took care of providing my family with a home and car. We did not fall behind in any of our bills. And during the last two months of my unemployment, we had a larger balance in our checking account than at any other time during our married lives. I still don't know how He did it, but He convinced me that He was worthy of my trust. Only then did He release me to accept a regular salary.

During those eight months, there were times when I would look at the way I had been treated by God and His people, whom I had faithfully served to the best of my ability, and feel that it simply wasn't fair. If I let myself dwell on the circumstances of my life, it was easy to fall into depression. But when I kept my focus on the word and vision of God, that I would become a more mature man of God with stronger faith in Him, how could I stay discouraged? Though the circumstances were not of my choosing and were in many ways unhappy, there was a purpose in it all! God was still in control and working for my good.

God has promised that the afflictions which come upon us will produce an eternal weight of glory, a lovely imperishable jewel. But that promise is conditional. The full purposes of God in our hearts will only be accomplished "while we look not at the things which are seen, but at the things which are not seen." We must take our eyes off the pain and focus them on the glory. We must look beyond the means and see the end. The sorrows of our life are only temporary, even though they may last for months or even years. Compared with eternity, they are but momentary.

In those times of pressure, during life's trying circumstances, we *need* revelation. We must ask the Lord what He is doing through this. We must have a vision which can carry us through to the other side. If we will listen for the voice of God, look for His vision, and hang on to what we receive, we need not be crushed with despair, but we can be overcomers, full of joy and the grace of God.

Unconfessed Sin

The knowledge that we have unconfessed sin in our lives, that we stand guilty before a holy God, can bring us into depression also. David spoke for all of us when he said, "For my iniquities are gone over my head; As a heavy burden they weigh too much for me (Ps. 38:4)." Unconfessed sin brings with it heaviness, depression and bodily sickness.

Why do we take so long to repent? Do we deceive ourselves into believing that indulging the flesh can give us lasting pleasure? Don't we realize that the flesh is never satisfied, but is an insatiable craving whose strength only increases with indulgence? Are we too proud to acknowledge our weakness before God and man?

Covenant within yourself that no longer will anything stand in the way of a clean conscience before the Lord. Commit yourself to daily and instant confession of every sin the Holy Spirit convinces you of. Wholeheartedly repent and receive the cleansing of the blood of Jesus. Be restored to the joy of your salvation.

If confession of all known sins still leaves you with depressive guilt, study again the chapter on the accuser and the Comforter. Make sure that you are not accepting false condemnation from the enemy who is trying to paralyze you with depression. Seek help from your spiritual advisor, if necessary, to help you discern the difference. Then walk in the joy of a purified heart!

Religiosity

Here we have come to the catalyst for the depression which

I struggled with for so many years. In my devoutness, before I had established a communion with God, I lived under an intense list of Christian rules which I believed were expected of me. I earnestly studied the Word and recorded every command and principle I found. I set out each day with that list before me, doing my best to conform to its standards. Whole areas of my life were cut off and discarded, bringing death to my personality and creativity. For example, living the Christian life was a serious undertaking and there was no time to play or have fun. Emotions were expressions of the soul, not the spirit (or so I believed), and therefore they were denied and quenched. Each day became a dreary striving to achieve approval from myself and God. And each day became a disappointing failure as I fell short of the mark. Depression became a constant enemy.

My Christianity had been reduced to religion. Like the Galatians, though I had received Christ through faith, I was attempting to live for Him in my own strength. Religion and Christianity are diametrically opposed to one another. Religion is a set of established rules; Christianity is a relationship. Religion stifles creativity; Christianity increases and releases the creativity of the Creator through us. Religion brings a heaviness to our spirits as we view the great task and our inability to accomplish it; Christianity brings a lightness to our hearts as we accept the strength of God to do His will. Religion is hard work; Christianity is rest and play, for we have ceased from our own labors (Rom. 4). Religion expresses itself in perfectionism, where I try my best to do what is right; Christianity is expressed in excellence, where I allow God's best to flow out through me. Religion breeds depression; Christianity produces joy.

How did I break free from the bondage of religiosity? When I learned to hear God's voice, I discovered Someone very different from the picture I had established in my mind. I heard

words of love and forgiveness and acceptance. I saw Someone
Who took time to be with His friends, play with children or
simply be alone and relax. Most importantly, I found Someone
inside of me who was not only able to keep the Laws of God in
His own earthly life, but He wanted to keep them through me!
I discovered that I could draw upon the flow of grace that was
living inside of me to overcome any temptation that came my
way.

If you are bound by the legalism of religion and walking in
depression, you can be free. Make contact with the Holy One
living inside of you. Listen to His words of truth. Look at His
vision of glory. Look up and rejoice!

Lack of Personal Discipline

Often we overlook this possibility in our search for a cause
for our depression. Especially if it is our normal way of living,
we may not recognize that there is another, better way.

If I do not have clear, divinely generated goals for my life, I
will find myself slipping into depression. I don't know where I
am, where I am going or if I am on the right path to get there. I
am on a road going nowhere and I want to get off. It is
imperative that I know what God wants me to do each day.
This is especially important for the self-employed, the
un-employed or the housewife. God may direct me to the
obvious tasks before me, but if I am commissioned to them by
God, I work under a sense of divine purpose and the most
mundane task becomes meaningful. This is not to say that I
must have a big prayer meeting before I can do anything.
Generally, if I am living in obedience to Christ and my heart is
fixed to serve only Him, the spontaneous flow of thoughts and
urgings are from the Lord. The point is to learn to be sensitive
and responsive to the spontaneous voice of God, not controlled
by the evidence that our physical eyes see.

Indecisiveness can also bring depression. We are faced with
an important decision. For weeks we waver back and forth

between the alternatives. Finally, under pressure, we make our choice, then spend the next few weeks wondering if our decision was wise. Our energy is drained and our spirits become depressed. Isn't there a better way?

When I must make an important decision, my first step is research. I read whatever I can find on the subject. I seek out men of God who are trained and experienced in the area under consideration and receive their counsel. When I am confident that I have all the data available, I bring it all into the presence of the Lord. Through journaling, I request and receive the leading of the Spirit of God. Since this is an important decision we are talking about, I will then submit what I believe to be the voice of God to my spiritual advisors for confirmation or adjustment. Finally, when I am satisfied that I have done all that God requires of me, I make my decision and act upon it. I do not allow myself to second guess, even if the results are not what I anticipated. I simply entrust myself to the One who has been leading me and who is able to work all things out for my good, even if I make a mistake.

That sounds like quite a time consuming project. What about decisions that must be made quickly? Then, I simply trust the Spirit who lives within me to give me wisdom for the need of the moment. There is always time to quiet the outward tensions and sense the still small voice of God within. Follow His leading to the best of your ability. Again, don't allow yourself to second guess. Even if you make a mistake, your God is big enough to somehow turn it to accomplish His will for your good. Trust Him.

Poor Care of the Body

Poor diet, exercise and sleep habits can all contribute to depression. There are some foods that bring a sluggishness to body and spirit. Overeating results in becoming overweight which contributes a poor self-image which breeds depression.

We need a vision of ourselves eating only to the glory of God and developing the healthy body God intended us to have.

Studies have shown that people suffering from depression will break free from its bondage twice as fast if they are exercising. Find out what kind of exercise routine the Lord has designed for you and draw upon His strength to carry it out. As your body responds, so will your spirit and the light of joy will begin to break through the clouds of depression.

Somehow the idea has found its way into Christian circles that the less sleep you get, the more spiritual you are. If you are out until midnight ministering and up again at four o'clock to pray for three hours, then you are a super saint. Maybe you *are* one of those people who need only four hours of sleep a night. If so, great! But most of us are not. Most of us will become over-tired and depressed if we try to maintain such a schedule. It is important that we have the freedom within ourselves to come apart and rest awhile. Sometimes the most spiritual thing you can do is go to bed and sleep. If you have more to do than you can fit into an 16-hour day, you are doing more than God wants you to do. Find out what *His* expectations are for your life and do only those things. Sometimes you even need a vacation. If you study the Old Testament laws, you will find that God established several times of feasting. During these celebrations, everyone was expected to leave their homes and daily routines and travel to Jerusalem for a giant "block party." True, there were spiritual obligations to fulfill, but the majority of the time was spent eating, drinking, dancing, playing and talking with friends. Don't be surprised if the Lord tells you you need a vacation sometimes, too.

Sickness/Physical Malfunction

Physical illness and disease can become the catalysts that plunge us into depression. There are several reasons this is so. Our bodily conditions have a direct effect on our spiritual condition. When physical sickness afflicts us, it is easy to fall prey to spiritual weaknesses of doubt, fear and depression.

One way that physical illness can precipitate depression is through a lowering of our energy levels. When everything we do seems to require more effort than we have to give, discouragement can set in. If our prayers for healing are not answered in the way we hoped, doubt can lead to despair. Particularly, long-term and recurring pain and suffering are fertile soil for the seeds of depression.

Chemical imbalances can also cause bouts of depression. Our emotions are closely tied to the chemical, endocrine and hormonal systems of our bodies. One reason exercise is so effective in fighting depression is that it releases chemicals into our bodies which promote a feeling of well-being. Many women find that during certain, predictable times they are immersed in the darkness of despair. If you can pinpoint the causes of these imbalances and recognize that they are temporary, it can help you survive until you see daylight again. During those days, baby yourself a bit. Take a bubble bath or relax in a hot tub. Don't accept any extra or unnecessary pressure or responsibility. Have your husband bring home supper. Don't make any rash decisions and avoid conflict if possible. Read a book and go to bed early. Chances are good that when you awaken, the cloud will have passed and you will once again be able to rejoice in the goodness of God.

There are some people who suffer on-going depression because of chemical malfunctioning or glandular disorders. I almost hesitate to even mention this as a possibility because it provides such an easy excuse for those who may not want to face the responsibility for their own emotional health. However, if you have examined your life carefully under the illumination of the Spirit and are totally convinced that you are listening only to the voice of God and seeing the vision of God, and yet depression holds you in its grip, you should consider the possibility of a physical cause. Earnestly seek God for healing, and if the healing tarries, receive the assistance of medical doctors to control the imbalance until the Lord corrects it. The abundant life is a life of joy, and God wants *you* to experience it!

Learning to Pray When You're Depressed

In Tim LaHaye's excellent book, *How to Win Over Depression*, he tells about a group of Christian college students who were suffering from depression. The group was divided into three sections. The first segment received group and individual counseling on how to improve their mental attitudes. The second group met together for prayer with a counselor who instructed them on how to pray properly. The third group was sent home to pray about their problems. The results were amazing. Group Two, who were guided in prayer, showed the greatest percentage of improvement. Group Three, who were simply encouraged to pray, showed no improvement and some even grew worse. This tells me that there are some ways of praying which are helpful to curing depression and some that are not.

Psalm 31 provides an excellent format for prayer for the depressed person. Although we will not write out the entire chapter here, I encourage you to read it through in your Bible.

My Bible labels this "A Psalm of Complaint and of Praise." At the time of its writing, David appears to have been facing several of the catalysts we have discussed. The circumstances of his life were trying, the weight of his sin was upon him and there are allusions to bodily illness. But in spite of all these negative conditions of his life, notice how he begins his psalm:

"In Thee, O Lord, I have taken refuge; Let me never be ashamed; In Thy righteousness deliver me. Incline Thine ear to me, rescue me quickly; Be Thou to me a rock of strength, A stronghold to save me. For Thou art my rock

and my fortress; For Thy name's sake Thou wilt lead me
and guide me...Thou art my strength..."

David does not immediately begin his prayer with a
recitation of his complaints. Instead, he turns his eyes upon the
Lord, focuses his attention on His goodness and blessings,
quieting himself before His presence. He gets his priorities
right. He declares forth his confidence in and commitment to
his God. He establishes proper focus right from the beginning.

In verse 6 he begins to allude to his problems, and finally, in
verse 9, he begins to present his sorrow and need to the Lord.

"...I am in distress; My eye is wasted away from grief, my
soul and my body also. For my life is spent with sorrow,
And my years with sighing; My strength has failed
because of my iniquity, And my body has wasted away..."

His life was not going at all well. Enemies were seeking his
life. Friends pretended they didn't know him. His name was
slandered through the land. The guilt of his sin weighed upon
him and his body was sick and in pain. Once he was in the
presence of God, he felt a freedom to express all his fears,
angers, hurts and sorrows. But he didn't stop there. If our
prayers are merely a rehearsal of our problems, there is no life
in them, only further death.

Once David had poured out all of his problems before the
Lord, he reaffirmed his trust in God to deliver him from them.

"But as for me, I trust in Thee, O Lord...My times are in
Thy hand; Deliver me from the hand of my enemies, and
from those who persecute me...Let me not be put to
shame...Let the lying lips be dumb..."

From verses 14 through 18, David tells the Lord how he would
like Him to handle the situation, always emphasizing that the
Lord is in control and well able to deliver.

Finally, in verses 19 through 24, David concludes his prayer with praise, faith, love and hope.

"How great is Thy goodness, which Thou has stored up for those who fear Thee, Which Thou hast wrought for those who take refuge in Thee...Blessed be the Lord, For He has made marvelous His lovingkindness to me in a besieged city..."

Only when we have touched God can the trials of our life be turned to cause for praise and rejoicing. Only when we have heard His words of comfort and wisdom, only when we have seen His vision of the joy set before us, can we come up out of the pit of depression into the sunshine of His joy.

Summary

The root cause of most depression is self-pity, which is a direct result of losing our divine focus and failing to see God. There are many catalysts which can contribute to our foray into the "sloughs of despond." Among the most common are life's trying circumstances, unconfessed sin, religiosity, lack of personal discipline, poor care of the body and sickness or physical malfunction. Every one of these "causes" can be overcome by returning to our divine focus by quieting ourselves, listening to the voice of God, seeing the vision of God and acting in obedience to it.

I do not claim that this chapter contains the total answer to the problem of depression. I only offer the answers which I have found so far that have been helpful to me and to those whom I have shared them with.

Response

Is depression ever a problem in your life? How persistent a problem is it? Are you able to see that you have lost divine focus at those times?

Are you currently suffering in depression? Were you able to

recognize the catalysts that plunged you into this darkness? Are you willing to come to Jesus, quiet yourself in His presence and allow Him to speak words of faith and hope and wisdom, restoring you to divine perspective? Do you want to see God in your life and circumstances? Do it now, and enter into the joy of your Lord.

Chapter Eleven

Victory through Death and Resurrection

Are there areas of sin in your life against which you have battled for a long time without finding consistent victory? Do the words "consecration," "holiness," and "self-denial" bring a sense of guilt and doom into your heart? Have you tried to present your body as a living sacrifice, only to have it crawl back off the altar? Do you ever wonder if the Christian message of freedom from sin is an empty promise with no hope of fulfillment? Does your heart echo the words of the Apostle Paul, "Wretched man that I am! Who will set me free from the body of this death? (Rom. 7:24)?"

"Thanks be to God through Jesus Christ our Lord! (Rom. 7:25)." There is a way of deliverance! The promises of the Word are always true. Freedom from sin and a life of holiness is available to the child of God. But there is only one way to find it. Standing tall in the center of Gospel, overshadowing every other doctrine and dogma, there is a cross. The death of Jesus, the holy, blameless Son of God, on the cross, satisfied forever the debt of our guilt and delivered us from eternal death. It was the only possible way.

We were with Him that day. We were crucified with Christ (Gal. 2:20). We died and our life was hidden with Christ in God (Col. 3:3). When we made Jesus Lord of our lives, philosophically, our decision was made. Positionally, it was done. Yet there remains this warring within our flesh. "The good that I wish, I do not do; but I practice the very evil that I do not wish (Rom. 7:19)." If I am dead, why do I act so very much alive?

There remains a personal cross which we must take up daily (Lk. 9:23). We must learn to consider ourselves to be dead to sin, but alive to God in Christ Jesus (Rom. 6:11). This is so important, for while death on the cross to all our selfish desires is an absolute necessity, it is not the final goal. Death is only a doorway, a means to an end. The ultimate goal of Christianity is that we may live in resurrection life, both now and throughout eternity. We have the glorious hope of the resurrection of our physical bodies to strengthen us through the terror of death and uphold us through the sorrow of mourning. In the same way, we have the hope of resurrection life in our mortal bodies to sustain us through the death of our old self, our body of sin (Rom. 6:6).

"For if we have died with Christ, we believe that we shall also live with Him...For the death that He died, He died to sin, once for all; but the life that He lives, He lives to God. Even so consider yourselves to be dead to sin, but alive to God in Christ Jesus. Therefore do not let sin reign in your mortal body that you should obey its lusts, and do not go on presenting the members of your body to sin as instruments of unrighteousness; but present yourselves to God as those alive from the dead, and your members as instruments of righteousness to God (Rom. 6:8-13)."

That I died with Christ on the cross is an absolute reality. My responsibility in dying daily is to remember this truth, reckon or consider it to be so, and call it forth in my life. When I look into the Word of God, I no longer see the Law standing in judgment over me. Instead, I see Jesus fulfilling the Law both in His own earthly life and out through me. I do not attempt to keep the Law through crucifying my own flesh, but I stand upon the fact that I have already been crucified. I do not war against the sinful passions which rise within me to tempt me to evil. Instead I turn my eyes from the fleshly desire and contemplate the reality that I am clothed with Christ, that the fullness of His life indwells me, that sin has no more power over me and I am free to live a holy life. And as I, "with unveiled face [am] beholding as in a mirror the glory of the Lord, [I am] being transformed into the same image from glory to glory, just as from the Lord, the Spirit (II Cor. 3:18)." If I set my mind on my sinful flesh and the apparent power that sin has over me, I will become frustrated and discouraged. But if I set my mind on the Spirit and His resurrection power flowing through me, strengthening me to conquer any foe, I experience life and peace (Rom. 8:6).

How can these theological ideas be put into practice in my every day life? When temptation strikes, how can I reckon myself dead to sin but alive to Christ? For example, suppose a friend whom I trusted betrays my confidence. My initial, instant reaction is hurt, which will express itself in anger and an urge to retaliate. This is my old self in reaction. So far, I have not moved into sin; I am just strongly tempted. At this point, I will not open my mouth or act in any way, because I know that if I do, I will sin since I will be acting out of myself. Instead, I will turn my thoughts inward, to Christ who lives within me. I will call to mind the fact that I am dead to personal responses. Though they may tempt me, they have no power over me to cause me to obey them. I will focus on Christ, who is my life, praying, "Lord, I feel hurt and angry. I have no power to forgive. But Lord, you are an eternal well-spring of love within me. You forgave even in the midst of deepest agony. Be to me now all that I need. Fill me with your love, your forgiveness, your understanding and your compassion. Consume with your grace all that would rise up against me." Sometimes gradually and sometimes instantly, there will come a release from the hurt and anger and a welling up within of the Spirit of Christ. When all my fleshly responses have been swallowed up in Jesus, I can respond to my friend with the character of Christ. I can become a minister of reconciliation and a messenger of peace.

I can go through this process in seconds, minutes, hours, months or even years. If I choose to nurse my wounds or cling to my fleshly responses to temptation, I will never move beyond my selfish reactions. If I focus on the temptation and its apparent power over me, trying to battle the flesh with the flesh, I will live in defeat. But if I will quiet myself in God's presence, express my need and weakness to Him, and allow Him to respond with words of grace and visions of victory, I will overcome. My automatic and spontaneous reaction to all of life must be to move quickly through each stage of death and resurrection. My ultimate goal of life is to live always in the final stage, standing peacefully within Jesus while walking through life.

There are three different perspectives I can have as a Christian. I can focus my eyes on *self, who is alive,* which is essentially living as a non-Christian. When temptation rises before me, I give in without a fight. Perhaps I have a false understanding of sin and believe that the immediate response of my flesh is an act of sin, and therefore, since I have already failed, I may as well complete the action. However, sin does not occur until I act upon the reaction of self. If I live with this perspective, I will live in self-effort, hurt, anger, retaliation, and self-will. I will experience anxieties, fears and extreme emotional ups and downs.

A second place I may focus my eyes is on *self, who is dead.* I will try to push the darkness of sin out of my life through my own efforts. I will become a religious zombie, reacting neither from myself nor from Christ. I will become lifeless, boring and very religious. There will be no spark nor personality, and there will be no place for fun, excitement, or joyous activity. My life will be centered on nothing but religious activities.

Obviously I am not recommending either of the above perspectives. Instead, I have a different focus, one of *Christ living within me*. Though I recognize that I am crucified and the old self is dead, I also acknowledge that I have been raised up with Christ and now am alive with resurrection power. When I see an area of darkness in my life, I drive it out by turning on the light, by bringing the presence of Christ into it. As a result, I begin to flow with the life of Jesus. I become loving, caring, full of faith, kind, wise and free. Because I am healed of my hurts, I can be used to heal the hurts of others. The character of Christ becomes manifest in me by the fruit of the Spirit. The power of Christ becomes manifest by the gifts of the Spirit.

Crucifying the desires of the flesh is not easy, nor is it fun. Let no one imagine that a life of sanctification and holiness can be entered into lightly. There will be pain and suffering. But if we will endure the cross, we will find a joyful release and freedom from bondage such as we have never experienced.

Jesus came to earth for the express purpose of dying on the cross. Before He began His ministry, He fasted for 40 days and overcame the temptation to find an easier way to fulfill His purpose. During His years of ministry, He was lauded as Messiah and King and offered the opportunity to sidestep the cross and establish His kingdom another way. Every temptation had to be overcome one by one, as over and over again Jesus affirmed, "Lord, not my will but Thine." Finally, on the night before His death, there came the hour of greatest struggle. He knew what lay ahead. He knew the price that had to be paid. There in Gethsemane, Jesus agonized in prayer until the flesh was overcome by the Spirit, and once again He affirmed, "Not my will but Thine."

Jesus did not wait until they threw Him down upon the cross to make His decision. He did not wait until the thorns pierced His brow to surrender His will. The battle was won in Gethsemane. Because He had prevailed in prayer, He was able to endure the cross.

We must also come to Gethsemane. Though we have made our decision early on to follow Him, we must repeatedly affirm our resolve in every aspect of our lives. Again and again, we must get alone with God and pray until our spirit overcomes our flesh and we can say, "Not my will but Thine." Then, when we face the cross and the fleshly desires must die, the battle will already have been won.

What happens at Gethsemane? We have our vision restored and our focus clarified. Often we come to prayer, knowing that we want to obey God and deeply desiring to do so, yet blinded by the desires of our flesh. As those desires loom so large before us, we may become focused on them and all that we are being asked to give up. Or we may see only the suffering that we expect to endure in order to become free. We may become so focused on the cross that we can no longer see the resurrection purposes of God beyond it. In Gethsemane, the Spirit will gently turn our focus outside of ourselves. He will show us the life of holiness flowing in resurrection power that will be ours. He will enable us to become like Jesus, "who for the joy set before Him endured the cross (Heb. 12:2)." Because of Gethsemane, we will be able to look beyond the cross to the resurrection.

Summary

"Truly, truly, I say to you, unless a grain of wheat falls into the earth and dies, it remains by itself alone; but if it dies, it bears much fruit. He who loves his life loses it; and he who hates his life in this world shall keep it to life eternal (John 12:24,25)." Death and resurrection are the keys to abundant life. If we cling to our life, demanding our rights and enjoying our sin, we shall lose it. But if we will give up our life, surrendering our rights and clinging only to Christ, we shall experience resurrection life. The fruit of righteousness will begin to grow and we will become a haven of peace in a weary world.

Response

Is the Spirit speaking to your heart about an area of your life which must be crucified? Will you find your Gethsemane, your place of prayer where you can pray through to victory? Will you listen to the gentle voice of the Spirit within you, giving you wisdom, understanding and grace? Will you receive the vision Jesus wants to instill within you of a life of holiness and purity? Will you cling only to His words and focus only on His vision, allowing them to lead you through death, into resurrection life?

that have given definition to their lives for years. For others, it has meant learning to say no to the multitude of demands which are made on their lives so that they may say yes only to Christ. For still others, it has meant time in Gethsemane, gaining the strength to endure the cross that they might live in resurrection victory over sin. For everyone, it has meant a restoration of divine focus, a renewal of our ability to see God and hear His voice in our hearts.

Now that we have come so far, how can we maintain a pure heart? How can we live free from the bondages that have held us in the past? Jesus said that the pure in heart shall see God. I believe the inverse is also true: that those who see God shall have a pure heart. Therefore, I believe the key to maintaining a pure heart is *seeing God everywhere.*

When I worship, it is easy to have a pure heart. I don't mean when I just sing; I mean when I touch the heart of God in worship. When I worship, I focus on the Lord and while I look, I become a reflection of Him. The problem comes when I turn from worship and look at people, events and the world around me. How quickly I lose my sense of His presence and power! Therefore, I must learn to see God everywhere I look.

I can see God as central to all matter because "in Him all things hold together (Col. 1:17)." I can see Him in all circumstances, for it is He "Who works all things after the counsel of His will (Eph. 1:11)." I see Christ as the center of all my spiritual attainments, because "by His doing you are in Christ Jesus, who became to us wisdom from God, and righteousness and sanctification and redemption (I Cor. 1:30)." I see Him as central to my life, my movement and my existence, for "in Him we live and move and exist (Acts 17:28)." I can see God everywhere, because He is everywhere. "Where can I go from Thy Spirit? Or where can I flee from Thy presence? If I ascend to heaven, Thou art there; If I make my bed in Sheol, behold, Thou art there. If I take the wings of the dawn, If I dwell in the remotest part of the sea, Even there Thy hand will lead me, And Thy right hand will lay hold of me (Ps. 139:7-10)." David had learned that even in the most horrible situation, even in hell itself, God was present and visible to the eye of faith.

The prophet Habakkuk spoke of a glorious day when the whole world would see as David did: "For the earth will be filled with the *knowledge* of the glory of the Lord, as the waters cover the sea (Hab. 2:14, emphasis added)." Notice, he did not say that a day was coming when the glory of the Lord would cover the earth. Indeed, that day is now here and has always been here since creation. Rather, it was a recognition of that glory, a knowledge of it, an ability to see the glory, that would cover the earth. When man fell, he lost his ability to see spiritual reality. When we are born again, we regain that ability, if we will but receive it. Therefore, our prayer must always be, "Open my eyes, that I may behold... (Ps. 119:18)."

God Revealed in His Creation

"For since the creation of the world, His invisible attributes, His eternal power and divine nature, have been clearly seen, being understood through what has been made, so that they are without excuse (Rom. 1:20)." There is so much of God that can be seen in what He has created. Though He is the Creator, He has infused everything He has created with His Spirit. If our eyes are open, we will learn divine truths through the four seasons, through the rain and the sunshine, through the birds and the animals. We will become better acquainted with our dearest Friend through seeing Him in His handiwork.

There are many marvelous Scriptures that tell of God's presence in nature.

"Listen closely to the thunder of His voice, and the rumbling that goes out from His mouth. Under the whole heaven He lets it loose and His lightning to the ends of the earth. After it, a voice roars; He thunders with His majesty voice; and He does not restrain the lightnings when His voice is heard. God thunders with His voice wondrously, doing great things which we cannot comprehend. For to the snow He says, 'Fall on the earth,' and to the downpour and the rain, 'Be strong'...Then the beast goes into its lair and remains in its den. Out of the south comes the storm and out of the north the cold. From the breath of God ice is made, and the expanse of the waters is frozen. Also with moisture He loads the thick cloud; He disperses the cloud of His lightning. And it changes direction, turning around by His guidance that it may do whatever He commands it on the face of the inhabited earth. Whether for correction, or for His world, or for lovingkindness, He causes it to happen (Job. 37:2-13)."

What a demonstration of His eternal power!

Jesus takes us to nature to give us a picture of His Father's divine nature.

"Look at the birds of the air, they do not sow, neither do they reap, nor gather into barns, and yet your heavenly Father feeds them. Are you not worth much more than they?...Observe how the lilies of the field grow; they do not toil nor do they spin, yet I say to you that even Solomon in all his glory did not clothe himself like one of these. But if God so arrays the grass of the field, which is alive today and tomorrow is thrown in the furnace, will He not much more do so for you...your heavenly Father knows that you need all these things (Matt. 6:25-34)."

As we see the lovingkindness and tender mercy God bestows on the most apparently unimportant creature in His world, we learn more about His unending love and care for us. As we see Him, our faith grows and our hearts are healed.

When David wanted to describe the invisible attributes of His God, He also turned to nature to find the right words.

"Thy lovingkindness, O Lord, extends to the heavens, thy faithfulness reaches to the skies. Thy righteousness is like the mountains of God; Thy judgments are like a great deep. O Lord, Thou preservest man and beast. How precious is Thy lovingkindness, O God! And the children of men take refuge in the shadow of Thy wings. They drink their fill of the abundance of Thy house; and Thou dost give them to drink of the river of Thy delights. For with Thee is the fountain of life; In Thy light we see light (Ps. 36:5-9)."

Only the immensity of His creation could begin to compare to the enormity of God's character.

Let our prayer continually be, "Open my eyes, Lord, that I might see Thee in Thy wondrous creation."

God Revealed in Spiritual Growth

Before I became a Christian, I believed I was in control of my life, making my own decisions, doing what I wanted. Though this was not true, for I was under the authority of the prince of the power of air, I was deceived into believing that I was the one in charge.

When I became a Christian, I carried that myth over into my new life. Because I was a follower of Christ, I would now obey Him and live a godly life, still in my own strength. It took me many years of frustration and failure to learn that natural man can never live a supernatural life. It is only through the power of the Spirit that works within us that the Christian life is possible. If I forget that I have died and Christ is now the source of my life, I will become wrapped up again in my efforts to keep the Law and lose the pure heart I have received.

Not that I no longer strive to be righteous, but now my striving is not according to my own power, but according to

His power, which mightily works within me, making me complete in Christ (Col. 1:28,29). Therefore, when I am called upon to keep His commandments, I take a step back into myself and call forth the only One who is truly able to do so. For example, John reminds us that "if we love one another, God abides in us, and His love is perfected in us (I Jn. 4:12)." We are not able to love one another through our own strength. If we are going to love, it will only be because of the love of God which abides within us.

If there is an area of spiritual growth which you are struggling to attain, come and yield your struggles to the One who is able and has already won the war. Recognize that you are but a branch, grafted into the Vine, supported and sustained by the life of another. Ask Him to open your eyes that you might see His hand at work in your life, conforming you into His image.

God Revealed in Everyday Work and Service
If only we could always be involved in worship and ministry! How easy it would be to see Christ then! If we believe that, then we are believing another lie of satan, that there is a division in life between the secular and the sacred. In Christ, there is no division. All of life becomes an act of worship for those who see God in all.

"Whatever you do in word or deed, do all in the name of the Lord Jesus (Col. 3:17)." Whether at home, on the job or in the church, everything I do is to be done unto the Lord. Wives, submit as unto the Lord (Eph. 5:22). Husbands, love as Christ loved (Eph. 5:25). Children, obey your parents in the Lord (Eph. 6:2). Fathers, bring up your children in the instruction of the Lord (Eph. 6:4). Employees, obey your employers as the Lord (Eph. 6:5,6). Employers, treat your employees right in the sight of the Lord (Eph. 6:9).

If you give a cup of cold water to the thirsty, you are doing it unto the Lord. If you give food to the hungry, you are doing it for Him. If you visit the sick or the prisoner, you are ministering to Christ (Matt. 25:31-46). If our eyes are open, He is everywhere, and everything we do is done unto Him. "Whatever you do, do your work heartily, as for the Lord, rather than for men; knowing that from the Lord you will receive the reward of the inheritance. It is the Lord Christ whom you serve (Col. 3:23,24)."

Let us pray that our eyes may be opened that we might see God in every facet of our lives, that every word we speak and every thing we do may be an act of worship to our Lord.

God Revealed in the Circumstances of Life

I do not believe it is possible for man to comprehend the fact that God has given men free will, and at the same time, He is working all things after the counsel of His will. Such a dichotomy of truth is beyond our ability to grasp. Thank God that He does not require complete understanding or even perfect theology, but only steadfast faith!

"God causes all things to work together for good to those who love God, to those who are called according to His purpose (Rom. 8:28)." "Having been predestined according to His purpose who works *all things* after the counsel of His will (Eph. 1:11)." We must have our eyes opened to the movement of the hand of God in every circumstance that surrounds us.

But, you may wonder, what about evil authorities and rulers? Surely God does not place them in positions of power! "For not from the east, nor from the west, nor from the desert comes exaltation; but God is the judge; He puts down one and exalts another (Ps. 75:6,7)." But what about their unrighteous judgments? What if they give rulings which are contrary to what God wants? "The king's heart is like channels of water in the hand of the Lord; he turns it wherever he wishes (Prov. 21:1)." Because I know that my God is bigger than any other ruler, I can confidently submit to every authority in my life. Through prayer, I have influence over every king, judge and employer. If I earnestly pray that God will guide their words and judgments, I can confidently rest in whatever decisions they make, knowing that their hearts have been turned by the Lord. Of course, if I have failed in my responsibility of earnest prayer and supplication for all in authority (I Tim. 2:1,2), God may allow ungodly rulers and poor judgments to be made so that I will be corrected and called back to my dependency on Him.

How easy it is to believe God is sovereign during the times of joy and peace! How hard it seems to accept that He is in control during sorrow and misfortune. But only by doing so can we maintain a pure heart and not be overcome with fear, doubt and anger. "I am the Lord and there is no other; besides Me there is no God. I will gird you, though you have not known Me; that men may know from the rising to the setting of the sun that there is no one besides Me. I am the Lord, and there is no other, the One forming light and creating darkness, causing well-being and creating calamity; I am the Lord who does all these (Is. 45:5-7)."

Not only must we see the hand of God in every circumstance of life, we must also hear the voice of God that we may know how we are to respond. Just because God has allowed a calamity to come into our lives does not mean that we are to passively accept the evil. There is a time to submit and a time to overcome. Only the voice and vision of God can give us guidance that we may know our proper response.

The people of Judah had been living in rebellion for many years. Again and again the word of the Lord came through His prophets that they must repent or suffer destruction. Yet they would not obey. Finally the day came when God's righteous judgment had to be satisfied. He spoke to Jeremiah saying, "Because you have not obeyed My words, behold, I will send and take all the families of the north,' declares the Lord, 'and I will send to Nebuchadnezzar king of Babylon, My servant, and will bring them against this land, and against its inhabitants, and against all these nations around about; and I will utterly destroy them, and make them a horror, and a hissing, and an everlasting desolation' (Jer. 25:8,9)." Because of your sin, said Jeremiah, this judgment is upon you. Therefore, submit to the power of the enemy, for he is acting as a servant of God for your discipline. When the time of judgment is passed, the Lord will turn and judge Nebuchadnezzar for being such a willing vessel for your destruction and you shall be restored. But for now, this is your discipline from the hand of the Lord. Therefore, submit.

But that does not mean we are always to stand powerless before the enemies of God. The prophet Elisha was in a similar situation to the people of Judah (II Kings 6:14-23). He was also surrounded by an enemy bent on his destruction. Yet he did not submit. Because he was a seer, he knew that God's plan for him was not submission but authority. Though there were only two in his house, himself and his servant, he said, "Those who are with us are more than those who are with them." His eyes were opened that he could see the armies of God and he spoke words of faith. The chariots of angels stood ready to consume his enemies, but they were under the authority of the servant of God. Therefore, when Elisha said, "Strike this people with blindness, I pray," the Lord moved in response to his prayer, and Elisha was the victor.

There is a time to submit and a time to conquer. We will only know for sure how we are to respond if we can see what God is doing in the situation and hear His words of guidance.

It is such comfort to know that God is in control, especially during the dark hours of our life. The most difficult times of my life so far have been times of transition, when God was moving me into the next phase of my life. The first time it happened, I didn't know what was happening. Every stable force in my life just seemed to disintegrate. Because I did not recognize the voice of God in my heart, I fell into doubt, anger and despair. Being a man of action, I looked around for a new position. Every option seemed closed to me except one. Because I could find no other choice, I pursued the only course open to me. I thought I was moving simply out of logic and necessity. Only later was I able to see the hand of God guiding and keeping me, even when I had no faith and the way seemed dark and aimless. What a blessing it was for me to realize that even though I had not seen it, God was still in control.

The next transition came in my life after I had learned to hear God's voice and see His vision. Again, all the circumstances seemed negative. Sometimes I would become depressed and think that other people were controlling my life and my future. But when I listened to the Lord through journaling, He assured me that He was in command of the situation and nothing could happen to me that He did not allow or ordain. He showed me when to speak and when to be silent, when to act and when to be still, when to submit and when to take authority. Though I cannot say I came through that time without any doubts or failures, I was more victorious than I had been the time before.

Right now I am again going through a time of change. It is certainly the guidance of God that has me writing this book during this time. Every day I have an opportunity to put into practice what I am recommending to you. I know that it works because it is working in my life day by day. I am doing better this time, I think. I have a greater confidence in the sovereignty of God than I have had in the past. When I seem to be treated unfairly, I have an assurance that no one can prevent God's will from being accomplished in my life except me. As long as I have a heart to do only His will and I keep my heart pure of anger and bitterness, He will turn hearts and circumstances to bring about His best for me. I am confident that no one has authority over me unless it has been given them from above

(John 19:11). Because I have become a seer, I hold before me a vision of what God has planned for me, and that vision carries me through the times of distress.

Whatever you are going through now, God is still in control. Ask Him to open your eyes that you might see His hand of love upon you. Open your ears that you might hear His words of truth.

Summary

"His name shall be called...Wonderful Counselor!" When our hearts are wounded, our spirits crushed, our minds clouded by doubt and despair, we have a Friend who loves us and offers us hope. If we will be still, listen, and look, He will speak words of healing and peace and give visions of joy and hope. When divine perspective is restored, our hearts shall be pure for we shall see God everywhere.

Communion With God — The Package of Materials

This is the most practical, down to earth teaching available in the world today training Christians how to dialogue with God. Over 99 percent of all participants begin to use vision in their prayer lives and write down pages and pages of dialogue with Almighty God on a regular basis. If you are not completely satisfied with this material and do not personally begin to receive and record the things the Lord is speaking to you, you may return this material in re-salable condition within 30 days for a **full money back refund.**

Communion With God Student's Workbook: a 150 page "write in" study manual. Mark Virkler teaches through this text on both the video and audio cassettes. $13.95

Communion With God Teacher's Guide: Twenty-two lesson outlines corresponding to the 22 video and audio sessions, laying the course out in detail for the leader/teacher. $11.95

Communion With God Video Tapes: 22 half-hour sessions of Mark Virkler teaching in a classroom setting. Purchase $299. Rental $99.

Communion With God Audio Cassettes: 22 half-hour sessions of Mark Virkler teaching through Communion With God. This corresponds exactly to the video series, except for an additional tape with four quieting exercises on it. $42.00

Dialogue With God: A 250 page teaching testimonial sharing not only the teaching of Communion With God, but also many pages of inspiring stories and testimonies. Included are 30 pages of journaling from individuals across several nations — a great source of encouragement for those beginning to journal. $6.95

Talking With Jesus: A 365 day devotional with Scripture and journaling for each day of the year. Evelyn Klumpenhouwer, the author, learned to hear God's voice in a communion with God seminar in Canada in 1986. This book stands as a testimony of the power of the message of Communion With God, to actually teach people to hear Gods voice. Tremendously life-giving. $7.95

Our Father Speaks Through Hebrews: A devotional of Hebrews by Rev. Peter Lord. Each journal entry has a verse from Hebrews followed by what the Lord spoke to Rev. Peter Lord concerning the truths in the verse. The first book of journaling produced by a man. Excellent, inspiring and life-giving. $7.95

Testimony

Dr. Richard Watson — Oral Roberts University

Communion With God by Mark and Patti Virkler has dramatically changed my prayer life. I have found I can will to dialogue with Christ on a daily basis, and I do. I believe this inspired approach to be absolutely essential to the growth of every serious Christian. I further believe **Communion With God** is an excellent example of the uniquely powerful way God is reaching out to His people today."

Rev. Thomas Reid — Full Gospel Tabernacle

"The course **Communion With God** is GOING TO CHANGE THE NATION by building a new generation of people that hear God's voice and dream God's dreams."

Spirit Born Creativity — The Package of Materials

The only book of its kind, teaching the process of releasing the creativity of God through the heart of the believer; subtitled "Making Dreams Come True." This 238-page book is ideal for businessmen, parents and anyone who wants to become more creative. Textbook $9.95; Teacher's Guide available $4.95.

Counseled By God — The Package of Materials

A revolutionary book showing you plainly how you can find healing for the basic emotional needs of your life by dialoguing through them with God. It deals with such topics as healing anger, fear, inferiority, and condemnation, allowing Christ to heal deep hurts from the past, and learning to incubate only God's voice and vision. If you have found the deep healing that comes as this book has guided you into interaction with God, you may want to obtain other supporting materials for either your personal use or for group use.

Counseled by God Textbook a 130 page stand alone trade paperback. Excellent for personal use. $6.95

Counseled By God Student's Workbook: A 130 page "write in" study manual. Excellent for group use. Mark Virkler teaches through this text on both the video and audio cassettes. $8.95

Counseled by God Teacher's Guide: Twenty-two lesson outlines corresponding to the 22 video and audio sessions, laying the course out in detail for the leader/teacher. $8.95

Counseled by God Video Tapes: 11 hours of Mark Virkler teaching in a classroom setting. Purchase — $299, Rental $99.

Counseled by God Audio Cassettes: 11 hours of Mark Virkler teaching through **Counseled by God**. This corresponds to the video series. $42.00

Mark Virkler is Available as a Seminar Speaker

Mark travels full time conducting Communion With God and other seminars at churches worldwide. Contact him at 716-655-0647 concerning arrangements to have him come to your church.

Testimonies

Rev. Peter Lord — Park Avenue Baptist Church

"I have been an active Baptist pastor for thirty-seven years. As far as I am personally concerned, seminars like "Counseled by God" and "Communion With God," and "Abiding in Christ" are absolutely fundamental to the building up of the inner life. At this present time we have six ongoing classes in "Communion With God" using Mark's video series and one class on "Counseled by God." I highly recommend him and his ministry to you. I would be glad to talk with you on the telephone if you have any questions." 407-269-6702.

Rev. Judson Cornwall, ThD.

"God has especially graced Brother Mark Virkler to help persons re-discover the art of communion with God. I have had the opportunity to observe this from a distance for a number of years, but I now have joined forces with this brother in seeking to get this teaching to an ever wider segment of the body of Christ.

"I would highly recommend Mark Virkler and his seminar **Communion With God** to all who still desire to do the will of the Father. His approach is both unique and God given. His integrity is well documented, and his value in bringing people into a depth of prayer cannot be over estimated."

Communion With God Ministries

Name _____ Phone _____

Address _____ City _____ State _____ Zip _____

Qty	Title	Price	Total
Communion With God			
_____	Communion With God Student's Workbook	$13.95	_____
_____	Communion With God Teacher's Guide	$11.95	_____
_____	Communion With God Audio Cassettes	$42.00	_____
_____	Communion With God Video Tapes		
	_____VHS _____Beta Purchase	$299.00	_____
	_____VHS _____Beta Rental	$99.00	_____
_____	Dialogue With God	$6.95	_____
_____	Talking With Jesus	$7.95	_____
_____	Our Father Speaks Through Hebrews	$7.95	_____
Counseled By God			
_____	Counseled By God Paperback textbook	$6.95	_____
_____	Counseled By God Student's Workbook	$8.95	_____
_____	Counseled By God Teacher's Guide	$9.95	_____
_____	Counseled by God Audio Cassettes	$42.00	_____
_____	Counseled by God Video Tapes		
	_____VHS _____Beta Purchase	$299.00	_____
	_____VHS _____Beta Rental	$99.00	_____
Cultivating Individual and Corporate Creativity			
_____	Spirit Born Creativity textbook	$9.95	_____
_____	Spirit Born Creativity Teacher's Guide	$4.95	_____
_____	What the Bible Says About Silver and Gold	$3.95	_____
_____	Twenty Key Biblical Principles for Christian Management	$9.95	_____

Shipping and Handling Charges		Sub-total _____
U.S. and Canada	8%	Shipping & handling _____
South America	13%	Total enclosed _____
Europe, Africa, Asia, & Australia	20%	

Please allow 6-8 weeks for delivery to overseas countries. COD available in U.S. only

Money Back Guarantee: If you are not completely satisfied with these materials, you may return them within 30 days in re-salable condition, and receive the full refund on the cost of the book.

Make **check payable** in U.S. currency to: **Communion With God Publishers,** 1431 Bullis Road, Elma, NY 14059. 716-655-0647

_____ A **free ordering catalog describing over 50 guided self discovery study manuals** (many with cassettes and videos) which Mark and Patti have developed. These are ideal for personal, small group and large group use, including home cell groups, Sunday school, Bible school, and Sunday and Wednesday evening church services. In addition to the above topics, this includes studies in the areas of abiding in Christ, Spirit born creativity, Christian dream interpretation, through the Bible series, creating and releasing wealth, worshipping with sign language, transmitting Spirit life, and much more.

_____ A **free** copy of **"In Touch"**, a magazine which keeps you informed of new materials and developments in Mark And Patti's ministry, "Communion With God."

_____ A **free** listing of 13 **seminars by Mark Virkler**, available to be hosted by your local church.